TRIUMPH
OVER
DARKNESS

Understanding and Healing
The Trauma of Childhood Sexual Abuse

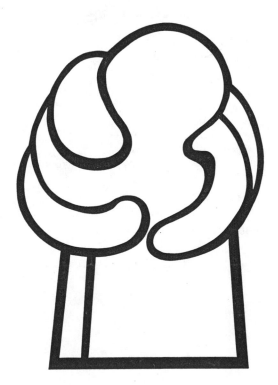

By
Wendy Ann Wood, M.A., and Leslie Ann Hatton

Published by:
Beyond Words Publishing, Inc.
Pumpkin Ridge Road
Route 3, Box 492-B
Hillsboro, OR 97123
Phone: 1-503-647-5109
Toll Free: 1-800-284-9673

The poems, letters, journal entries, drawings and other
accounts in this collection were sent to the authors to be
published as recovery readings on incest, rape and abuse.
Most of the poets have allowed us to use their names. The
names of other contributors have been omitted to preserve
the privacy and anonymity of the contributors and their
families.

Printed by Arcata Graphics, Kingsport, TN
        in the United States of America
First printing May, 1988
ISBN: 0-941831-15-9
Library of Congress Catalog Number
        88-070819

Book design by David Forester
Illustrations by Spencer Lewis
Jacket design by Gary Lund

A Dedication

To each of us who is on a path of healing.

ACKNOWLEDGEMENTS

When this project began it was only a dream. Over the past five years it has become reality. So many friends have helped us along the journey, both with the development of the actual contents of the book and also by giving us emotional support. Their encouragement has kept us moving through the intensity of the feelings being shared. At times during this journey, our hearts would hurt and we would become overwhelmed with the impact of the pain that was brought before us. It was then we found strength from those around us.

I, Wendy, would especially like to thank my friend Steve, who serves as a sounding board, shows me my own inner strength, and helps to guide me along life's path. To my parents, who have supported me unconditionally through thick and thin my whole life, I want to give my appreciation and love.

I, Leslie, would like to express gratitude to Vicki, my therapist and friend, who has taught me about the light. She has offered me the grounding I need; she is my mentor. A special thanks to my husband, Jim, who gave up many hours of time and attention to *Triumph Over Darkness* without complaint. Also, to my step-children Abra, David, and William, I express appreciation for their enthusiasm about this book and their sacrifices for it. My little boy, Ryan, was born when this project began. He deserves special thanks for his patience and cooperation while Wendy and I worked intently on the book. I convey my gratitude and respect to my parents, who have been a source of inspiration and who taught me the values of life.

Stella Logan, R.N., gave us a boost of energy many times during this project and spent hours reviewing submitted material. She has been with us since the beginning and has offered faith and support in us and this work.

To Bruce McCulley of Cavalcade Productions we give thanks for his time, travel, expertise, and friendship.

Richard Cohn, our publisher, has been great. We appreciate his excitement, knowledge, insights, and humor. He has pulled this work out of our closets, and produced the reality of our hope.

A special thanks to Paul Dagle and Michael Morgan, who gave of their time and counsel on the legal aspects of this book.

Words cannot express enough our appreciation to David Forester and Spencer Lewis for their unconditional devotion and creative energy to complete this book.

To Allison and Jim Allison for their design and graphic layout on the ECHOES NETWORK, Inc., brochure, Jerrie Thompson for the many hours of duplicating, Wes Wait and Jean Wright for introducing us to Richard, we say thank you.

We have heartfelt gratitude for each person in our individual support systems: Bobbi Sachs, Ph.D.; Lenna Burkinshaw, M.A.; Hugo Maynard, Ph.D.; Karen Fryar; Sally Fitts; Jerri Olsen; Diana Carlson; Marlene Bachelder; Sue Duffield; Tami Stephens; Ellen, James, and Callie Pritchard; The Growth Group; Sparkle; Michelle McAllister; Monica and Todd Powers; and Christine Hatcher. Thanks for all the little things that mean so much.

A special thanks, as well, to all who were willing to open their lives so the pages of this book could unfold.

And to each other we say, "Let's go to the beach!!"

PREFACE

Does anyone hear me? Can anyone feel my pain? Am I all alone with the intensity of my emotions? Is it normal to feel this way?

When groups of people gather to discuss childhood sexual abuse, they typically cover myths, facts, statistics, and clinical aspects. Yet something seems to be missing. Amid all the talk, one senses unspoken feelings that are being shouted out, but only by the heart. Yes, something is missing — the reality of the feelings of those who have been abused.

Through more than a decade of work in the area of sexual abuse, we saw and heard the deep pain that people continue to suffer after having been abused as children or adolescents. As we began to realize just how needy so many of these people are, we wondered what people did to recover and move forward in their lives.

Many former victims search local bookstore shelves for a hint from some text that the emotions they feel are "normal." They need to know they are not alone in this struggle, and that others have experienced and overcome these traumas. But most literature on sexual abuse is limited to either clinical research by practitioners or surrealist versions of an individual victim's story. Scarce indeed is material that could help adult victims get in touch with their feelings and go through the necessary stages of accepting and healing.

A more intimate and personal means of sharing, we felt, was urgently needed. We searched for a way to communicate the wide spectrum of emotions that are normal during the recovery process. We also wanted to bring together the experiences, emotions, struggles, and healing processes of people who had been sexually abused, and to share with others who have had similar life experiences. So three thousand brochures went out to clinics, therapists, resource centers, crisis centers, and individuals all over the United States. These invited former abuse victims to share their experiences, how they have survived on a day-to-day basis, and what has helped them to heal.

Looking back, it seems we were unprepared for the emotional impact the outpouring of responses would have on us. The writings brought up depression, sadness, anger, and myriad other emotions. In producing this book, we used most of what we received and did not change any accounts to make them sound "nice" or "proper." Thus *Triumph Over Darkness* evolved with our desire to help those of you experiencing trauma, and those in recovery, to become stronger through an honest sharing of "gut-level" feelings.

We realize that recovery from sexual abuse is a process; those who read this book will be at different stages along the way. We portray this healing process so you will know the wide range and levels of emotion that occur, that they are "normal" and can be worked through.

Hopefully our readers will also include family members and friends of abuse victims. They, too, suffer emotional pain in the aftermath of sexual abuse of a loved one. Perhaps they can gain some insights, information, and empathy for the struggles that make survivors out of victims.

To former victims we wish to stress: Whatever happened to you, do not minimize your emotions by comparing the pain of your experiences, or the stage of recovery you are at now, with that of others. Your feelings are real and valid. As you share these many different accounts of others' abuse situations, we hope you will see that the healing process takes time and must be gone through at your own pace. We also offer the sharing presented in *Triumph Over Darkness* as a source of encouragement and support. There is hope and there are people who understand.

Some accounts in this book are difficult to read, even overwhelming; others may leave you feeling angry, depressed, and hopeless; and some share healing, growth, and strength. For the contributors to this book, *Triumph Over Darkness* has been a safe place for releasing the intense emotions they feel.

Please realize this is not a replacement for therapy. People who are still living with the pain of sexual abuse need a place to let feelings flow without fear of judgement, disbelief, or rejection. Finding a supportive, caring person whom you can trust is very important in getting the feelings out. It is our hope that *Triumph Over Darkness* will also help serve you in this purpose. We feel it is the truth that heals. Painful secrets need to be released and the truth must be told. Then we can be free to go on in a healthy way — to live and not just to survive.

INTRODUCTION

There is something wonderful about touch, especially for children. After a long day at school a hug says, "Welcome home, sweetheart, I love you!" The squeeze of a hand on the way to the doctor's office can mean, "It's all right, I am right here with you." When a rough and tumble game of family football is done, a pat on the back says, "You did a good job!"

In today's world, where our children grow up so quickly, we need to use touches like these to remind them that they are special, that we love them, care for them, accept and support them. After all, isn't that what we all want from those around us?

But what about touches that leave a hurtful impression on a child for a long, long time? That is what sexual abuse does. It inflicts invisible scars, sometimes for life.

Being abused sows images and ideas that often create deeply rooted feelings of anger, distrust, and revulsion towards sexuality. Perhaps for this reason, among others, our society has chosen to ignore and thus avoid the reality of childhood sexual abuse.

Yet sexual abuse is real, and it impairs the lives of hundreds of thousands of children and adults every year. It not only damages the child victim, but also the offender, the non-offending parent and the entire family. It also affects the former child victims well past their childhoods as they, now grown, must continue to deal with the day-to-day impact of the childhood trauma.

The purpose of this book is to help you understand and accept the reality of the physical, emotional and spiritual pain that sexual abuse creates. We especially suggest *Triumph Over Darkness* be used as a tool in therapy to help you get in touch with your own feelings as you move toward healing. Be assured: this book faces the impact of sexual abuse squarely. We believe that one needs to experience his or her feelings, old or new, deal with the reality of those feelings, and then go on to heal the scars that no one sees but that are so deeply felt.

Bringing out of the shadows the heretofore secret feelings of abuse victims may also assist therapists, parents, spouses and all others who really care and want to help stop the continuing effects of abuse. Perhaps this book will play a role in preventing the children of today from experiencing the trauma of abuse.

But above all, it is meant to offer support and encouragement to those who have already experienced abuse and are ready to take bold steps out of the darkness and into the light.

Just as this has not been an easy book to write, for most it will not be an easy book to read. So we encourage you to put on warm slippers as you walk through this work, realizing that at times you may also need a soft blanket, a cup of tea, and a hand to hold. Some of the entries may seem difficult to integrate. Trust your inner self to help pace you on this walk. Sometimes even take off your warm slippers to rest and soak your feet.

The book is divided into two parts: 1) the darkness and fear that come from the trauma, and 2) the light and hope that are found in recovery. We have included individual writings from others' experiences where they fit along the continuum of healing. At the end of each chapter our insights and perceptions will offer you some grounding.

We look forward to the day when a book such as this will be obsolete. Until then, it is our desire that *Triumph Over Darkness* will be a resource of light to guide you through and out of the fear and darkness to discover the beauty that lies within, beyond words.

STATISTICS

Let's begin by taking a hard look at the facts. First you should know that according to a Congressional Committee report, 50–80% of all sexual abuse cases go unreported in the United States.

One in three women have been sexually assaulted, by someone they know, by the age 13 (*F.B.I. Uniform Crime Reports,* 1982).

One in ten males have been sexually assaulted, by someone they know, by the age 13 (*F.B.I. Uniform Crime Reports,* 1982).

29% of offenders are strangers to the child (*Men Who Rape,* Groth, N., Plenum Press, New York, 1979).

Between 1980-1984 there has been a 459% increase in reported child sexual abuse crimes.

In 75 to 85% of the cases reported, the offender is someone known to the immediate family (*Surviving Sexual Assualt*, Grossman, R., with Sutherland, J., Congdon & Weed, Inc., 1983).

97% of the offenders are males and 3% are females.

70% of young prostitutes and 80% of female drug users were sexually abused by a family member (*Best Kept Secret*, Rush, S., McGraw-Hill, 1980).

74% of offenders have one or more prior convictions for sexual offenses against a child (Groth, 1979).

31% of child sexual abuse involves penetration.

82% of the offenders committed their first offense when under 30 years of age (Groth, 1979).

21% of the child sexual abuse victims are females between ages 7-11 years.

The median age of children who are sexually abused is 11 (*Against Our Will,* Brownmiller, S., Bantam Books, 1975).

40% of sexual abuse occurres over a period of time ranging from weeks to years (Brownmiller, 1975).

In 60% of the cases force or assult was used (Brownmiller, 1975).

More heterosexual males sexually abuse other males than homosexual males (Mann, D., Lecture Notes, 1988)

Male victimization involves more male-to-male sexual contact than femal-to-male (Mann, D., 1988)

60% of sexual assult occurs in the home of the victim or offender (Grossman, R., 1983)

MYTHS AND FACTS

The process of demythologizing sexual abuse means addressing those myths that have been used as an excuse to avoid the real issues of the abuse. As these myths show, many seem to have been created and propagated by the child molesters themselves. By taking a close look at these myths and facts about child sexual abuse we can begin the process of breaking down the strong denial system that seems to go hand in hand with the secret.

MYTH: *The child is lying or making up stories.*
FACT: Most children do not have the knowledge or sexual vocabulary to make up explicit stories about sexual abuse. Always believe a child when he or she is disclosing something about sexual abuse. To not act, and accuse the child of lying, could be detrimental and even life-threatening, especially if this unheeded disclosure is discovered by the offender.

MYTH: *The child was being seductive.*
FACT: Oftentimes a child molester interprets a child's need for attention, nurturance and affection as seductive. Child pornography portrays children as sex objects and as provocative. Children do not know how to be overtly seductive unless it has been taught to them by the offender. Oftentimes a child behaving in a seductive manner is a warning sign that the child has been molested. The responsibility to openly address seductive behavior, and not act on it, belongs to the adult and not to the child.

MYTH: *The child likes it.*
FACT: Often the only attention a child gets is when the actual incest is taking place. The child likes the attention, but does not like the sexual manipulation. This often brings with it feelings of confusion about what the differences are between love and sex, which in turn results in guilt.

MYTH: *Mothers usually know about and approve of the incest.*
FACT: 55% of the cases reported are reported by the mother. Once reported, often the mothers are confused and as powerless as their children in dealing with the incest. Sometimes the mother has unmet dependency needs, is sexually withdrawn from the husband, or was abused herself and is therefore unable to objectively see what is going on in the home.

MYTH: *The incest offender is an alcoholic or addicted to drugs.*
FACT: Studies show that somewhere between 10% and 33% of incest offenders are alcoholics. Little has been found in the relation of incest to drug addiction.

MYTH: *The child is not harmed by incest and it has little, if any negative impact on the victim.*
FACT: Two-thirds of children who have been sexually abused experience immediate emotional disturbance. Long-term results indicate that psychological disturbances are higher among victims than non-victims. This is especially true in the areas of depression, character disorders, anxiety and guilt reactions, sexual dysfunction, self-mutilating behavior, homosexuality, and dissociative disorders. Medical traumas including genital injury are numerous. Pregnancy and sexually transmitted diseases also occur in incest victims more often than one would like to believe.

MYTH: *The offender is just a sexually frustrated dirty old man.*
FACT: Most offenders and rapists have other sexual outlets. Misusing their power and authority is their way of gaining control over other people. It is impossible for incest to be consensual because of the unequal power structure between the adult and the child.

MYTH: *Incest only occurs in lower socio-economic groups.*
FACT: Offenders are found in all social classes, races, and religions. Their yearly income falls within the national median.

MYTH: *It will only frighten and traumatize children to openly discuss child sexual abuse with them.*
FACT: Sexual assault must be presented as a safety issue. Vague warnings like "Don't take candy from strangers" and "Don't let anyone ever touch you" can often confuse and frighten children. If sexual assault is presented correctly, it should be no more frightening then talking about car safety, how to cross the street and planning the household fire escape route. We have to train our children, and avoiding the subject can be unforgivable.

The myths and facts can be hard to look at, but they do give us some hopeful insights. Allowing the myths to continue is continuing the lie. Let's not get trapped in the myths. We now know the facts and can take those facts to where they need to be: to our children.

TABLE OF CONTENTS

PART 1
FROM THE DARKNESS

CHAPTER ONE: **A PAINFUL TOUCH**

CHAPTER TWO: **HOLDING ON**

CHAPTER THREE: **PANDORA'S BOX**

PART 2
INTO THE LIGHT

CHAPTER SEVEN: **ECHOES FROM THE DARKNESS**

PART ONE

FROM
THE DARKNESS

A PAINFUL TOUCH

"'Hi, Mr. Jenkins,' she said, feeling that she needed to be polite to him since he was her mother's neighbor. Suddenly, she felt a pair of hands stroking her body and before she knew it, Mr. Jenkins was kissing her sloppily on the lips and then she knew that something was wrong."

Minerva M.

IN A CHILD'S EYES

She had walked down those same streets for ten years now, always in the same fashion, clinging to her mother's skirts because that was all she had. Her father had left a few years before and she wanted to make sure that her mother wouldn't think it had been her fault.

On hot summer nights, she and her mother would sit outside on the stoop while her mother spoke to the neighbors and she watched the other children play, but she couldn't join them. She needed to stay close to her mother always. Seventy-year-old Mr. Jenkins came over often to chat. His presence appalled her. She would stare at his face and arms which were all burned, stained and ugly and wonder what had happened to him, fearing that something like that would happen to her. *No!* Her mother was there to protect her, she thought.

The only time she separated from her mother was to walk the poodle in the grocery store downstairs. She loved the poodle and enjoyed taking care of him. The store was pleased to have such a diligent little worker on hand to assist in the care of the dog. Mr. Jenkins always promised to buy her one and often gave her money for candy and toys which she never knew whether she should accept or not.

One day her mother was too busy to go out with her as usual, but encouraged her to go out and play with the dog anyway. She excitedly skipped down to the store, thrilled with her freedom. She went into the store and went straight for the storage room where the dog was usually tied. There wasn't much light in there, but she sensed someone enter the room behind her. It was Mr. Jenkins.

"Hi, Mr. Jenkins," she said, feeling that she needed to be polite to him since he was her mother's neighbor. Suddenly, she felt a pair of hands stroking her body and before she knew it, Mr. Jenkins was kissing her sloppily on the lips and then she knew that something was wrong. She turned around and ran out of the store, leaving the dog behind and the memory of that figure looming over her. When she got outside, she felt a wave of nausea making its way up her throat and she began to spit repeatedly on the ground, hoping to get rid of the sour taste left in her mouth, but she knew it would never leave.

She ran home and into her room and thought and thought. Her head throbbed with confusion. Her mother had warned her about men who tricked little girls with candy. She recalled her father kissing her mother the same way. She wondered if that was why her mother had sent him away and then she understood.

Minerva M.

PROGRESS REPORT ON MINERVA

It has now been two years since I was raped and fourteen years since I was sexually molested. There were many occasions which were fraught with anguish and despair; the process of recovery has been a long and painful one. It is also these very experiences which have shaped the person I am now. Without these experiences there would not have been the drive and ambition to overcome and strive for more. True, there were many times when I just wanted to crawl into a corner and die. Still, I had dreams that I couldn't lose sight of and those kept me going.

I am now a certified Social Worker at age 24 and am building a career working with child sexual abuse and rape victims. Now I am able to use these experiences to help others; turning poison into medicine.

To have been able to write about these experiences, for you to read, has had a curative effect on me. Supportive family and friends are invaluable in the recovery process. Seek out anyone who will listen and express your feelings openly. Nothing will prevent us from moving forward more than suffering in silence. Gradually, in this manner, anger will transform into strength and pain into growth. Eventually we move from victim to survivor. Healing is a lifelong process, and the pain will go away as long as we never lose hope for the future on account of our pasts.

GAMES

She was little. So very little. And small. Inside, too. Her very youngness was a threat. It reminded him that he was getting old. It mocked the dried-outness of his useless life, that freshness of hers. He wanted some of her life, her joy for himself. He wanted to possess it. He wanted to possess her.

It started out innocently enough — on her part. In her trust and adoration she saw nothing strange in them shedding their clothes. She revelled in the freedom from restraint and with hilarity and abandon leaped and giggled just in her own skin.

Over days and weeks and months, the game increased in scope. Touching games escalated into serious business. More and more was required and she found she had to work — to perform — whether it was fun anymore or not. And somewhere in the seventh month it stopped being fun.

The familiar horsie game, the sensuality of flying high, of being the queen of all the land, making her big daddy her slave, developed a subtle twist. The illusion of the control she thought she had was slipping. More and more her Prince Valiant overrode her queenly decisions. More and more the game went on past her decree to stop.

And then, in that awful seventh month, her decrees became awful, wrenching pleas. The prince became a great, fire-breathing dragon. He breathed into her very being a horridness and vileness that choked her and made her retch but not cry out.

Not yet.

And he laughed. And he reached inside her and pulled out her joy and her trust and her sense of her very self and he ate them up and vomited them all over her cringing, fearful little body. He was enraged that her joy had not become his own, that it refused to stay inside him and he turned on her in a fury which unleashed the devil in him.

He beat her with his fists and when she did not cry out, frozen with fear, he cursed her and shook her and knocked her into walls and furniture.

And with a single cry, a hardly-heard moan, her frozen fear melted into a gray daze of protecting clouds, a thin attempt to stretch over the deep wound in her spirit. And he dropped her on the floor at his feet.

When he walked away from her, the despoiled joy that had once been hers returned in a sinister, evil form. It mocked her and tormented her with hissing, vile sounds that made this tightness of her skin a prison out of which she could never escape. Those sounds became her jailers, their monotonous gyrations enveloping her, seducing her, freeing her from peace and enslaving her in their merciless tyranny.

Even though *he* walked away. And left her on the floor. They *never* will. They never will.

Janet Wood

PROGRESS REPORT ON JANET

I am not completely recovered, and I don't know if recovery from something so traumatic and devastating can ever be termed "complete." Certainly the horror of it will never be entirely erased. Yet I am better than I have ever been before. I am continuing to heal hour by hour, day by day, and week by week.

In my case healing is coming by a combination of things including: prayer, God's healing and a very wonderful psychologist. I am able to talk about the past traumas, including the feelings associated with them. As I do, I am beginning to be free of them.

The journey isn't over yet, but I can see the light at the end of the tunnel. I no longer consider suicide daily. I no longer hurt myself with razor blades or bruising. I seldom slip into the deep, dark despair that used to be my closest companion. I am better, much better, and I thank God for that.

THE RETURN

The horrors return
in the night
in my dreams
in my reality.

The smell
of old booze
and garlic
Your hot breath
smelling up my room
telling me to be quiet
holding me down.

I struggled
you tried to kiss me
slobbering, pungent.
I held my mouth closed tightly
my legs even tighter
gripping my thighs together
my ankles intertwined
Leave me alone.
I'll show you what it's like
Fighting back, scratching.
Then the pillow
over my face,
I was smothering
I was dying . . .
groping hands
pulling my legs apart
pain, horror,
betrayal . . .
Raped . . . yes daddy, you showed me what it was like.

Pamela J.

PROGRESS REPORT ON PAMELA

So much has changed in my life. After sending off the writing I put it away, the incest, the memories, the pictures, the feelings, in a tidy little box hidden in the closet. I was so sure I was finished with it and could get on with my life. For the next two years I continued to drink and use drugs to block the feelings and the fears, until I hit bottom. I was an addict and an alcoholic who was tired of running. I placed myself in a very intensive treatment program where I dealt with my alcohol and drug problem and with some of my incest issues. I have continued to remain clean and sober for sixteen months through active participation in a 12-step program.

For the first time in my 34 years on this earth, I am involved in a healthy relationship. This has prompted me to pull out these writings and take a good look at how putting my incest in a box tied up with strings was not the way to heal myself.

I entered therapy again with the same therapist I'd seen years before. Today as a clean and sober woman I can face the fears of my past. I am just beginning to discover Pammy, that little girl who got lost so long ago. She is the key to my reconciliation to myself. I embrace her, forgive her, believe her, and love her.

I've discovered that healing is a process. Before, I wanted an instant cure and sought to alleviate the pain through alcohol and drugs. My healing is ongoing and each day I remain open to it, it happens. It is scary sometimes but well worth it. My running days are over. I've hung up my shoes. Sign me, healthy and happy.

CRIB STORY

She was crying, alone and afraid in her crib, the bars protecting her from freedom. She thought everyone had gone and left her alone with the gathering dusk.

She heard heavy footsteps coming down the hall. Her heart beat wildly, rising almost to her very dry mouth. Her bedroom door opened and it was her dad. She didn't know whether to be relieved or more frightened.

He lifted her stiff self out of the crib without a word. And brought her into his room. The shades were drawn, the big bed rumpled, the sheets dingy. The shadows and dust made the air seem thick with a suffocating grayness.

He shut the door and put her in his bed. He placed his cigar on the dresser and slowly undressed, not looking at her. He stood naked beside the bed. A giant of flesh and fearful nakedness. He turned to her and began pulling off her clothes, her stiff form yielding as he growled at her resistance, her fear melting her bones.

Then he touched her, and she stiffened again. He spread her legs and put his finger inside her, stretching her until it hurt, stretching her until she made herself go limp so he could play his game and get it over with, then she could go back to being a little girl. *If* she could. *If* he would let her.

He rubbed his fingers all over her bathroom place, making funny little noises that made her sick. He called her nice names that made her feel dirty and wicked. He told her she had to say she loved him, so she did but she had to fight not to cry. If she cried it would be worse, much worse. She learned that last time.

He pushed on her stomach and put his fingers back inside her, "making room," he said. She thought of the plastic furniture from her doll house and wondered if he were going to play house inside her. She hoped not, but whatever it was, she wanted it over fast. It was hurting more than usual but she knew she had to keep her body limp or it would be worse. Much worse.

His hands rubbed over her whole body but mostly on her thighs. His voice got gravelly as he crooned. Little bits of drool coming from his mouth dripped on her but she repressed a shudder, knowing what would happen.

The gray shadows deepened and she heard her mother call somewhere inside her head, but she wasn't really there.

Her father groaned. His daddy-thing grew huge coming at her like a snake out of a thicket. She grew stiff with terror and this time she couldn't make herself limp. She knew that thing was going to hurt her and she struggled to get away but she couldn't. She cried and pleaded, but he ignored her. He pulled her hair so hard her face stretched and he pinned her down. She couldn't breathe or cry or move and he forced his thing deep inside her again and again and again. The deep grays turned to black and as he came out of her she felt her life trickling out of her down her legs. She knew the pain had killed her and that she would never move or live or breathe again. She knew she would die right there because the pain was so bad. She knew she had nothing left inside her. She was empty. She was dead.

She was wrong. She was sorry she was wrong, because there was no escaping the daddy-days in his bed. And it got worse. Much worse.

Janet Wood

CHILDHOOD ECHOES

It was a bright, sunny day when my father decided to go up to my grandfather's. He was going to paint the house white. He left me inside the house with my grandfather.

When my dad went home it all started. It seemed so mysterious. My grandpa said, "I will take her home." He started to give me orders and was sweet to me. Then one thing led to another, he was feeling and touching me. He made me do things so he could masturbate me in my genital area. His hands were rough and cigarette-stained. It felt so unpleasant and strange. He kept saying, "You're my special girl, don't tell anyone, this is a secret." He then made me lie down, he blindfolded me and then he had "sex" with me. It felt real slimy. Then he played doctor with me.

After that he said he would take me home. We drove to a busy intersection. Then he pulled his car in at a store to get a bag of M&M's to reward me. I thought we were going home but instead headed towards his house again. He took me inside, took off my clothes and felt my breasts. He did that about three times. When it got dark, he finally took me home. He drove down a curved road and stopped by a pink house with a windmill in front of it. Then he made me put my head towards the door and took off my clothes. He proceeded to masturbate me again.

It was five o'clock and dinner was waiting. I felt an echo of silence which turned into hatred.

Anonymous

Some nights, it would hurt so damn bad, I didn't think I could sur-
vive the pain. The sexual part was devastating. I always felt so
"used" and unclean. But the beatings with his leather belt would
leave me trembling with fear for hours. I didn't cry. He wouldn't let
me. All I could do to comfort myself was to curl into as tight a ball
as I could and try to forget it happened. I didn't know what else to
do. After all, I was only twelve.

Anonymous

LISTEN TO ME

He corners me during the day, Mother. The nights

I wake screaming, you bend

like a slow axe, your braid loosening

across my cheek. You want to believe me.

You sit on my bed fingering a stray thread,

Your left eye twitching. I call you, Mother,

when he reaches around my back for my hands.

He keeps licking his lips. I stiffen against the wall

that snags my dress, any word

but his tongue, Mother,

his tongue in my mouth.

Susan Lorraine Madonich

I WAS A VICTIM

Things began to change as I started in school. I really didn't like what was happening, but I couldn't stop it. I was afraid to.

It was a normal day. I went to school and I came home from school. I went up to my room to change from school clothes to play clothes. Tim came upstairs and was standing in the doorway watching me. He went over to the bed and sat down. Then he had me come over to the bed and had me take my pants and underpants off. He made me lay down on the bed. He got on top of me and he put his penis in my vagina. It hurt so bad. It hurt to go to the bathroom. He started doing this every day.

Then one day it changed. I was at school and I was waiting for my mom to get home so I could go home. The last time I called home, Tim said there was a big box on the steps for me from my real dad. I thought, "*Wow!* A present from my dad and it isn't even my birthday!" So I walked home and as I came up to our house I didn't see a present or anything. All that was there was Tim. I went up the steps into the house, and straight up to my room to change. He followed me. He stood in the doorway and watched me change; then he came over to the bed and sat down. He made me sit on his lap for a couple of minutes. Then he put me down and made me take my pants and underpants off. He made me lay down on the bed, with my legs bent up and apart. Then he got on the bed and started licking me. I heard a noise. I told him we were going to get caught. It was Ed, my stepfather. He stood and watched until Tim was done and then he started in. I cried through it all. They called me a baby. Ed gave me money. I felt like a hooker — a whore, a slut.

After that day, it was repeated, intercourse one day, the other the next day. These things happened from first grade to fourth grade. Then he was put in jail.

Next is Louie. Some nights he would make me masturbate him, other nights it would be sucking. That was gross. I always threw up from that. Then one night he made me have intercourse with him. It really hurt. It felt like he did it on purpose. He would make me bleed. I would cut my arm with a razor blade so my mom wouldn't think anything about the blood. If I wouldn't let him do these things, he would hit me with his fists until I did let him. Intercourse would happen mostly on the weekdays and the other things would happen on the weekends. These things happened for a little over two years. It stopped only because he had to go to prison. His reason for making me do those things was that he had to practice for his girl friend. He wanted to be perfect for his girl friend.

A lot of things continued to happen with Ed, my stepfather. He made me french kiss him. He started fondling my breasts. He would always come up behind me and put his hands on my breasts under my bra. Sometimes he would put his mouth on my breasts. It hurt because sometimes he would bite them. I remember two times he made me have intercourse with him. Once he made me suck his penis in the shed outside. These things happened for almost five years. It stopped because I finally told and it finally stopped.

Judy
Age 17

PROGRESS REPORT ON JUDY

I am me and I am okay!

I am 20 years old now and have been in therapy for the last four years. I have come a long way but still have a long way to go. It would have been a lot easier if I'd had a loving and caring family supporting me, but I didn't. I do have a lot of great and caring friends to whom I can turn when I need someone, and a therapist who is behind me one hundred percent.

In therapy right now I am dealing with my past. Saying what happened out loud, and feeling those feelings I wouldn't allow myself to feel as a child. I am finally starting to get angry after all these years. Life can be hard at times, but I am going to make it!

Sometimes I feel like nothing. But, I know now that even though I feel that way, it isn't true. I am a survivor of something awful, but I'm worth something great. I am me and I am okay!!

WHAT MY FATHER TOLD ME

Always I have done what was asked, the melmac
dishes stacked on rag towels, the slack
of the vacuum cleaner cord wound around my hand,
the laundry hung limp from the line.
There is much to do always, and I do it. The iron
resting in its frame, hot in the shallow pan
of summer as the basins of his hands push
the book I am reading aside.
I do as I am told, hold his penis like the garden
hose, in this bedroom, in that bathroom, over
the toilet or my own stomach. I do
the chores, pull weeds out back, shuffle
through stink bug husks and snail
carcasses, pile dead grass in black bags.
At night his feet are safe on their pads, light
on the wall to wall as he takes the hallway
to my room.
His voice, the hiss of lawn sprinklers, wet
hush of sweat beneath his hollows, the mucus
still damp in the corner of my eyes as I wake.
Summer ended. School work didn't suit me.
My fingers unaccustomed to the slimness
of a pen, the delicate touch it takes
to uncoil the mind.
History. A dateline pinned to the wall.
And beneath each president's face, a quotation.
Pictures of buffalo and wheat fields, a wagon train
circled for the night, my hand raised to ask the question,
Where did the children sleep?

Dorianne

FOOTSTEPS

I'm awakened by the creaking of the floor. Footsteps. Someone is coming in the darkness. I close my eyes tighter, hoping if I squeeze them tight enough the footsteps will disappear. I pull my blankets closer, holding them tensely under my chin. I feel myself sinking into my bed as I draw my knees up close to my body. Sink, I wish I could keep sinking down into the darkness. I desperately want the dark and its softness to wrap around me and pull me down inside, swallow me up and take me away. My heart is pounding so loudly it is impossible for me to hide. His hand touches my back and reality jolts my body like an electric shock. I am sickened knowing it is happening again.

Anonymous

LITTLE REMINDERS

Remember

how I asked you

how I begged you

for that
brown plastic
leather looking
shoulder bag
at the store

You know

the one that was on sale
for three dollars

A Blue-Light Special

Remember

how you got mad at me

that same day

choked me

with that same purse

Reminding me
who was in charge
who paid the rent
whose food I was eating
and
that you had even bought me a purse

I remember

and

I never asked again.

Donna McGrew

INSIGHTS AND PERCEPTIONS

After reading this chapter, you may be left with the rawness of your own emotions. Some of these feelings may be new, while others may be resurfacing after having been put to rest for many years. Maybe at this moment you feel you would rather not re-experience or deal with this pain. But doing so can get you started on your journey toward wholeness — a journey that simply has no shortcuts.

Dealing with intense emotions and experiences often weighs us down with a sense of hopelessness. It is okay to feel the despair and pain, because what happened was not okay in any way, shape, or form. Let yourself feel the pain, fear, anger, or any other emotions that arise. Your feelings are valid. Accept them for what they are. Perhaps it would help to share your feelings with someone who is able to listen. Writing, shredding paper, drawing, even scribbling your feelings may also help release some of the intensity. Listen to your inner self and respond as a friend.

BE ACCEPTING

CHAPTER TWO

HOLDING ON

"I hate living for the most part. I've considered suicide time after time. The only thing that has stopped me is the kids."

Roberta

ROBERTA'S STORY

I've only talked about my experience once, and not in full. I'm not sure exactly what to tell, or even if I can. But I'll try — to help the children.

My name is Roberta. I am 33 years of age. I have two children, in their mid-teens, who have lived with me and whom I have solely supported and cared for since their birth.

My abuse took place in Portland, Oregon, by my stepfather. Well, he was just living with my mother; I thought they got married in 1958, but they hadn't. So, I guess he wasn't really, legally, my stepfather. He was just a huge, mean alcoholic who not only sexually abused my older sister and me, but physically and mentally abused my two younger brothers and mother as well.

The first time he sexually abused me was when I was in second grade. He did so repeatedly, every chance he got, until I ran away from home when I was 14. Sometimes I could hear him abusing my sister in another room. He beat us daily, whether we needed it or not. Life was pure hell. My mother never knew — or if she did, she certainly never let on to the sexual abuse.

No one in our family was close, never hugging each other. I can't ever remember my mom hugging me until I was 18 or 19 years old, and a few times since. As much as it hurts me to say it, I don't hug my children. I hate myself for being like my mother in that aspect. It hurts so much to not know how to show love and give love willingly. It feels like my thoughts and feelings get choked up and won't reveal themselves. Sometimes, in fact most times, I don't know how I feel. Just bitter and confused, cold, alone and scared.

You asked how I deal with anger, guilt, self-image and fear. I live from day to day, dealing with my emotions totally differently each day. No two of my reactions, on the same subject, will be the same. Some days, I can smile. Most days I feel worthless, defeated and very angry.

I hate living for the most part. I've considered suicide time after time. The only thing that has stopped me is the kids. They would have no one if I were gone and then, sometimes I feel they would be better off with foster parents or someone who can give them a better life. You see? Total confusion in my brain.

After my stepfather began abusing me I became very withdrawn. We weren't allowed to socialize at all, except at school. So I put everything into my school. I got A's and B's easily. I was so afraid that someone would find out what my stepdad was doing, and I would have died of humiliation, so I wouldn't talk. In class, if I were called on to answer or say anything, I would be so afraid I literally wet my pants at my desk seat.

I didn't have many friends, as you can probably guess. My stepfather would have killed me if anyone had found out. So I kept quiet.

Anyway, I'm very angry most of the time. Angry about the way my life was and is. I hated being a child and being so vulnerable to someone who only wanted to harm me. I hated him fiercely. I hated my mother for not knowing! How could she possibly not know what was going on for seven or eight years? How could she not see it in my eyes or see it in my withdrawal? My God, if my daughter was being abused I would know. Now I speak to my mother about one time a year, if that. My stepfather died in 1981.

How do I handle the guilt? I handle it by feeling guilty about *everything*. I am my own worst enemy. I hardly ever look in the mirror, I hate myself. And, I'm not ugly. I have been told more than enough that I am quite pretty. I have a weight problem that developed when I was nine. Since then I have gone from

130 pounds to 170 to 104 to my present 165! I hate being fat. But I eat because I am depressed. I always stay home except to go to work, and right now my health isn't permitting me to function at work properly.

I deal with fear now pretty much the same. I'm constantly afraid to let my feelings show. I should say, my good feelings. It doesn't bother me, until afterwards, to get pissed off, to yell and cry for hours. Then I feel guilty for showing such terrible emotions.

I'm afraid if I look good, I'll be more vulnerable to men and I don't want to be. I haven't had a boyfriend for over a year and if I stay heavy I don't have to worry about it.

I fear people talking about me, looking at me. I hate going shopping, even for groceries. I won't go to a bar, but I'll drink at home alone. I sleep approximately three to four hours per night. Most of my sleep is filled with nightmares, teeth grinding and crying.

I quit wetting my bed at the age of 12. My stepfather used to wake me up before he left for work, at six in the morning, to see if I wet my bed. If I had, which was six out of seven times, he would grab my hair and rub my face in it.

He used to make my sister and me pull our panties down in front of him to see if we were wearing clean panties. Perverted didn't even describe him. He should have been put to death for the pain and agony he has caused all of us. I'll never tell my mother. She wouldn't believe me anyway. She doesn't care. She always looked the other way.

Being an abused child leads to a very disturbing adulthood when one doesn't get the proper care to understand it. I feel it's too late for me. I'm very, very tired of even caring.

I write poems, and they're all sad. I can't even think of nice things most of the time. I feel I just exist. How can you have much respect for someone who's 33 and acts 12 or 13?

I just started seeing a counselor and I can't tell yet if it is going to help. I feel like it is my last hope. My kids will be gone and grown within four years; what am I to do? I feel like my entire purpose in life is going to leave with them. They're all I've had that's decent, and I feel I've failed them deeply.

Roberta

PROGRESS REPORT ON ROBERTA

The healing process is very long and difficult. Sometimes when I least expect it, a memory will flash and the fear and pain will come again. I've come to realize that the abuse will always affect my life. I am who I am because it happened to me, because I survived. I have since gone on to use those painful times for my good. Counseling and the support of loving, committed friends helped me the most to overcome my fears and helplessness.

Another part of my healing process has been for me to tell my story. It seems that for each person who listens and supports me, another lie is overcome and more silence is broken. The most difficult part of the process was confronting and dealing with the people who abused me; and those who allowed it to occur by their own fears and silence.

Counseling gave me the power to stand up for myself, whether it meant walking away, saying something or saying nothing. I no longer have to placate those around me. I am valuable and worthwhile in my own right.

Ronalda's Story

I am 24 and most of my life I have been fighting to hang on, and not give up. I was raped by my father when I was three. I grew up watching my mom get beaten, cut up, burned and run over. My mom used to beat me and lock me in closets. Finally all four of us kids were dropped off at a home with notes on our chests.

Two years later my mom showed up remarried to Johnny. I was six, and for six years till I was 12 I was molested and left in fear of men. My mom sent me away to my father, and I was raped again — by my father. Then the court took me and it was hell. In one of the halfway homes one of the men approached me.

I was raped again when I was 20 when I was a cocktail waitress.

Now I have a wonderful son. I have to get help so I won't hurt my son. I was always the victim, and I am still a victim. I hope someday it will stop. I am currently trying to get help with getting my anger out. I can't seem to get it out. It scares me. Men — I'll always hate them. And I'll hurt them back some day.

Ronalda

How Can I?

How can I see the sky so blue
When all I see is clouds?
How can I hear the robin sing
When I can't cry out loud?
How can I see the sunshine
When all I see is rain?
How can I smile and sing with joy
When all I know is pain?
How can I trust you daddy
When you hurt me like you do?
How can I love you, Mommy
When you just look right through?
How can I love somebody
When all I feel is hate?
How can I have a future
When my past I can't escape?

Roberta

THE BETRAYAL

"Janet!"

She awakes with a start, the urgency in the voice compelling her to return from sleep, and she knows she had heard her name being called even in her sleep, and she knows she must respond. But to whom? And to what?

Obedient to she-knew-not-what, she hurriedly puts on her knitted slippers and her pink flannel robe.

She keeps her bedside lamp on, but doesn't turn on the brighter overhead lights as she cautiously creeps down the stairs to the main floor. Listening, her heart pounding, her ears throbbing, her whole body pulsing with fear.

At the bottom of the stairs, she reaches the door. As she turns the knob to open it, she feels pressure from the other side. Her knees turn to water, her mouth fills with cotton and her head is fuzzy, her mind uncomprehending. All she knows is fear. There never existed anything before it and nothing will exist but the fear forever after.

She is suspended for a moment — an eternity — when her father's voice comes through the door. "Janet? What are you doing there?"

She tries to answer but there aren't any words in her head. Her mouth opens and shuts. She is shaking. Hard.

"Open the door." His voice sounds impatient. She knows she must obey. Her hand is still on the doorknob. She concentrates all the power and strength in her body to enable her to turn the knob again.

This time there is no resistance and she slowly pushes the door away from her.

He's not there. She stands for a minute afraid to step down the last step to the floor; more afraid of what will happen if she doesn't.

She has to know where he is. She can't get close, but if she doesn't know where he is, he'll sneak up behind her and scare her more than she can stand.

Closing the door behind her, she tries to have pillowed, silent feet as she creeps down the hall. In the living room she sees a familiar glow and she is flooded with relief.

"Mommy!" She runs toward her mother who is sitting on the couch, smoking a cigarette. Her mother pushes her away roughly, throwing harsh words at her.

"You slut! You whore! If you go looking for trouble, you'll find more than you bargained for! I can promise you that!"

Her mother's angry words fill Janet with confusion and hopelessness. There is no one left.

Her mother stands abruptly and stomps into her own bedroom. Janet stands stunned, unmoving. She is aware of her father in the dining room. The deadness in her chest which came from her mother's words is quickly being swallowed up by the all-too-familiar terror.

His breathing gets louder as he leads her into the basement. It's black. The old black sofa bed creaks hideously as he opens it up. She knows there are spiders and snakes hiding in the recesses but she knows better than to say anything. She knows that nothing she says will make a difference. The terror of what is about to happen and the terror of the creepy things and the terror of the basement itself begins to recede, as the gray clouded padding fills up her body and her mind and she goes far away inside herself, so that she doesn't know what his hands and his mouth and his teeth do to her. She isn't aware of him moving inside her like a huge ugly snake. She doesn't have to feel the enormous guilt that threatens to engulf her very being because she isn't there. Just her body. And that doesn't count.

Janet Wood

Jan Huson

DONE TO YOU

Done to you
Done to you
Many things were
Done to you
They were dirty
They were bad
All those things they
Did to you.
You held on
And went along
With all those things they
Did to you.
But you had no idea to run away
There was no place to safely play
Those black marks on your soul would stay
If you dared a word to say.
A bad, bad girl, you'd burn someday
If you fought those things that were
Done to you.

Rylee Brown

PROGRESS REPORT ON RYLEE

"Rylee Brown" is the pseudonym used by this 36-year-old survivor of sexual and ritualistic abuse. In 1986, explaining years of illness and puzzling symptoms, she was diagnosed as having a Multiple Personality Disorder, stemming from the trauma of her abuses.

For the past three years Rylee has worked closely with a psychologist, and together they have uncovered the secrets which have tormented her for so long. In now seeing and understanding the basis for her illness Rylee and her psychologist are beginning to help reach and heal her many personalities.

Writing in journals, composing poetry and music, rekindling a relationship with God, and meeting and developing relationships with other abuse survivors helps Rylee in her daily struggle to overcome her early traumas. Rylee lives in Oregon with her husband and four children.

Abuse: A Blight On Our Success

This is a story of three women and what they think they deserve out of life. The first woman does not think that she deserves life at all. The second woman doesn't believe she deserves to be in the world, and the third woman does not believe that she deserves money, power, recognition, respect and love. In short, she thinks she does not deserve success.

These women have three things in common:

1. They all are women who must work for their own economic survival.
2. They all have suffered abuse.
3. This abuse has been obstructive to their vocational achievement.

The abuse varied in its intensity and horror. Some was abrupt and traumatic, as in Dolly's case. Dolly was raped, shot, beaten, and run over by a car.

Some was continuous and occurred over a long period of time, as in Betty's case. Her former husband beat her intermittently throughout their 25-year marriage.

Some abuse happened long, long ago in childhood, buried under layers of denial and forced forgetfulness. This is Susanna's situation. Her grandfather made her suck his tongue in open-mouthed kisses. This occurred between the ages of four and ten.

The abuse may vary in its intensity and horror, but it has one effect. That is the destruction of self-esteem, and with the destruction of self-esteem comes the thought that we do not deserve life or love or money or a good job or respect or power or all those things together. That somehow women are born to suffer, to have less, to not need as much, to occupy less space. That somehow we, as women, do not deserve to revel in life and all of its abundance. That somehow we are life's victims, and so it shall be forever.

We struggle to be decision makers. But we get confused and sometimes we even say that rape, battering, and incest have nothing to do with our business and professional lives. However, the reality of abuse in our lives creeps over us like a blight rotting our self-esteem, destroying our self-worth, eroding our self-confidence.

Some of us do not recover, and we fail. That is Dolly's story. Dolly was working at her clerical job, overtime, one night almost three years ago. Two men broke into her office. They both raped her. They also beat her, shot her, and ran over her with their car. Incredibly, Dolly is still alive, if we can call Dolly's life living. The quality of her living eerily fits my dictionary definition of blight: "A blight is a disease or injury of a plant resulting in withering, cessation of growth, and death of the parts without rotting."

Dolly's gunshot wound is healed; the broken ribs mended; the bruises faded; the black eyes gone. The quality of her skin and the sweetness of her smile make Dolly one of the most beautiful young women I have ever seen. But there is a blight inside of Dolly. She is withering. She has ceased to grow. She is still beautiful, but the signs are there — a kind of listlessness, a dryness at the corner of the eyes. She tells me that she doesn't eat. She whispers that she is dehydrated.

Languidly she sits before me in my office. It has taken a month of phone calls, mailgrams, and pleading from her attorney, and finally she has arrived. She has been referred to me for vocational rehabilitation services. My job is to help her return to the working world. She has not worked since that terrible night more than two years ago.

I know what to ask, because I have her medical and psychiatric reports and I know her behavior. She dreams and drifts on the chair before me. I ask, "Dolly, what did you take before coming here?" Obediently she replies, "I shot up cocaine. Took two valium, and I had a drink."

"Dolly," I tell her desperately, because I hope I can catch her, "Dolly, in order to work with me you have to be clean."

"I know," she says compliantly, and tears come into her beautiful eyes.

I found drug programs. I had her call them while sitting at my desk. I made her promise to call me, but all the while I had the sensation that I was speaking to a wraith, a ghost — that Dolly had already died and that all my intentions and good deeds were useless.

Dolly told me about how she lives. She sleeps as much as possible, and when she's awake, she takes drugs — any kind of drugs. I ask her how she can support her habits. It turns out that the drug dealers give her drugs in exchange for sex. I asked her if they had put her on the street yet. She said no, and I believed her, but it was only a matter of time, as the blight did its work aided and abetted by the drugs. Dolly's youth and beauty were withering. Dolly had received a $20,000 Workers' Compensation settlement, but she gave it away to a former boyfriend. She said, "I was stoned at the time."

But Dolly knows that she doesn't deserve to have $20,000 of her own. She never came back to me either, because Dolly knows that she doesn't deserve to have a job of her own. How could Dolly believe that she deserved those things when what Dolly knows best of all is that she doesn't deserve life itself?

Another definition of blight is something which impairs or limits, and this results in the "getting by" response to abuse. This is what a 25-year marriage to a violent husband has done to Betty. Betty lives in a two-bedroom apartment with her boyfriend. The curtains are drawn, and the walls are covered with seascapes and paintings of mountains and lakes. The corners are stuffed with bric-a-brac. The tables are littered with books and papers. It is as though Betty is trying to stuff the world in, instead of going out to it.

Her harem mentality is expressed in other ways common to battered women. She is afraid to go downstairs to the park across the street. She does not have a driver's license. She does not own a car. She does not know how to drive. She is marooned and utterly dependent in one of the world's largest, wealthiest and most vital cities.

She is 46 years old and has the appearance and personality of a kewpie doll. She had a part-time job as a retail sales clerk. Her boyfriend drove her the six blocks to and from work. She injured her neck lifting heavy merchandise, and she was referred to me so I could assist her in finding less physically demanding work.

Now Betty has headaches every day and her neck hurts all of the time. I understand Betty because I had managed to catch a lonely sentence in her psychological evaluation. It said, "The patient was frequently beaten by her husband of 20 years." And that was it.

There was no exploration of effects of this continuous violence on Betty's mental and emotional state. There was no paragraph outlining the destruction of Betty's self-esteem and her fear of the world. There was no mention of the impact this violence might have on Betty's ability to get a job. There wasn't a word about how Betty's work-related injury is probably a way for Betty to finally receive sympathy and support for all that unresolved, unacknowledged, unknown, and unrecorded pain she endured all those lonely, hidden years.

I have learned to look for those lonely little sentences in medical reports, because I estimate that 90 to 95 percent of the women referred to me as the result of work-related injuries are also victims of rape, battering, or incest.

I was able to get Betty out of the house long enough to go to a trade school to learn medical receptionist skills, but when it came time for the job search effort, Betty put up her walls and withdrew. She's working part-time at home for her boyfriend, who has a contracting business. She's using her skills, but like the affluent women of the Middle East, she is behind walls, behind the veil. She is a purdah.

Betty has chosen the "getting by" response to abuse, because she doesn't think she is good enough to be in the world.

A blight is also something which frustrates plans or hopes, and so we come to the third category of response to abuse in our lives: achieving. Is this not the most ironic of conditions? Just when we thought we had stuffed all that hurt and all that rage and all that self-hatred down really deep and very, very far away ("I've banished it!" we say to ourselves), hoping that nobody will notice how sad and lonely and afraid we really are. We cover our hurt with success. We are the first person in our family to graduate from college. We are the best athlete. We get our Ph.D. We are the "Outstanding Woman of the Year," the president of our professional association. We are "supermoms" and other wonders of our suburban neighborhood. We get jobs no other women have ever held. We are water walkers in the large corporation. We get promoted quickly to a powerful position as manager, right under the vice president. We are in charge of 33 people.

This is what happened to Susanna — young, bright, well-educated, enthusiastic, a team player, a hard worker, and in two years the manager. Three months later the job was gone. Susanna was fired, bitter, unemployed. Her staff divided and hostile to her. Friends lost. Self-esteem at an all-time low. Gaunt face, pain etched around her mouth.

"My jaw aches. My teeth hurt. I can't sleep." She is haggard. This, the shining, confident, cheerful woman I have adopted as a mentor — now devastated.

"What happened?" I asked her.

"It feels like rape," she responds, and I believe her. Then I begin to remember all the little warning signs over the past weeks. A sense of doom about her, as though her failure was inevitable and irrevocable now that she had achieved her goal. A sense of implosion. A building up of inner tension and chaos twisting my young friend like an evil hand, and she — helpless within its grip. Finally implosion and collapse from within, and explosion and expulsion from the treasured job and even the company itself. The blight again frustrating hopes and plans.

The blight again, but what is it? "It feels like rape," she said, and yet she had not been raped, and she had a loving husband. For a while, it looked as though she had it all, but disease was there waiting all the while, despite all Susanna's protestations that what had happened between her and her grandfather wasn't much, wasn't important.

"I mean compared to other people. After all, he just made me suck his tongue."

"Susanna," I said her name very gently. "Susanna, I'll bet you wanted to bite his tongue right off, didn't you?" Her hands flew to her mouth.

"My jaw!" she cried out in astonishment. I nodded at her.

"That's right. It's not an accident that your jaw and teeth hurt right now."

Together we figured out that little Susanna, who was forced to suck her grandfather's tongue for hours on end, from age four to ten, could not endure receiving respect, recognition, money, and status as expressed in the new job. Little Susanna knew her worth. She knew that she was worthless and so when all the good things of life began flowing towards her, just as the adult Susanna had hoped and planned for, there was an inner chaos so unbearable that the real Susanna, divided between terrified, humiliated, and isolated child and the achieving, powerful adult, collapsed. She imploded.

She knew better. She knew that she didn't deserve the fullness of life. How dare she raise above herself? She knew what life was. It was fear. It was not trusting anyone. It was being ignored and abandoned just as Mommy and Daddy ignored and abandoned her. It was being molested. Most of all it was being there, without being there.

Being there as a hard worker, an overachiever, a slave even. Running so fast that nobody will really notice — and then to be the center of attention. To have 33 people hang on every word. To have 33 people acknowledge, notice, and worst of all — watch. This cannot be, because then the secret is revealed. The taboo is broken, and the taboo of incest is so powerful that it does not allow the victim to appreciate her own experience. It is a curse which scarcely allows her to remember the experience, let alone ponder it, discuss it, bring it to light, and heal it. Even the process of revelation is humiliating. It is as though she must endure the agony of it all over again. Nonetheless, the incest experience festers in a life like an infection or a blight, and this is what happened to Susanna.

This is how abuse is a blight on our success. This is why as women we have not achieved our vocational potential. Rape, battering and incest create self-hatred and lack of self-confidence which is so deeply rooted that we have only begun to design the appropriate treatment modalities to heal ourselves.

If we are the decision makers, we will continue this process and accelerate it. Because heal ourselves we must. Otherwise we will remain hostile, rebellious, resentful, dissatisfied, weak, unrealized, unfulfilled, and not deserving, instead of creative, powerful, assertive, wealthy, loving, bold, and deserving.

The decision is ours.

Patricia Ann Murphy

INSIGHTS AND PERCEPTIONS

This chapter has shared stories of survival, examples of how people hold on and cope when life seems unbearable. As an abused child, you probably found some way to insulate and protect yourself from the trauma. This constant need for self-protection often causes the child to suppress real emotions and, instead, to become numb (create an alternate feeling). These survival techniques may carry over into adulthood.

At this point, if you are willing to take a risk, try to look at yourself to see what feelings you might be smothering. Allow yourself also to examine what you have been doing to survive. Which methods are self-defeating, and which are positive and healthy?

It is all right to use the survival resources you've developed. Do not judge yourself; they served a valuable purpose at one time. Maybe as you grow, you will find you no longer have a need for them. Hold on to yourself and allow others to hold you, too.

BE COMPASSIONATE

CHAPTER THREE

PANDORA'S BOX

"'Pandora's box locked away for many, many years. Hidden secrets of days to be forgotten. Brought to life, so that yesterday begins to feel like today."

Crystal Ann Jordan

THE SOFTEST HANDS

I am a female, 40 years old. My two sisters and I were sexually abused by our uncle, around when I was three and four years old. We would stay over at their house sometimes for days. My uncle would come into our room at night, and take one of us up to his bedroom. My aunt slept downstairs so he waited until she was asleep. All I can remember is his carrying me up the steps; after the last step I can't remember anything after that.

This went on for a couple of years, till my dad remarried when I was five. We still went over there and saw my aunt and uncle but we didn't stay overnight. As I remember back then, I liked my uncle. He was small and thin, but he had the softest voice and hands; I think they are what I remember the most. I liked being over there; it was comfortable and nice and warm. But I blocked it all out. I only found out a few years ago that when my uncle was younger, he was in prison for five years for raping an eight-year-old girl.

When I was growing up, it seemed like something was missing from my life. It was like I didn't have any childhood, like I was so much older than the other kids my age. When I was in grade school I didn't talk to any boys at all. Sometimes at night I would lay in bed and think about my sexuality, and play with myself, and I always wondered why it felt so good.

In high school I started to date, but it was always with older boys. When I was 16 I was engaged to a 26-year-old guy. I would never let any one of them touch me. I got married at 17 to someone that looked older than he was. I remember the first time we had intercourse I kept thinking, Is this all? There has to be more to it.

He wanted to know who else screwed me before, because he said I was no virgin. He wouldn't believe me when I told him he was the first one.

He never did satisfy me. After six months of marriage I started going out on him and kept it up for the next 18 years. We had three children, but I still messed around. It seemed like I was always looking and searching for something I never found. I would have one-night stands or affairs that would last two or three years. My husband knew I was going out now and then, but he loved me, so it was like he turned the other way.

During that time I took an art instruction course. My favorite pictures I did for years were portraits done in charcoal of little girls with sad faces. I guess it reflected back on my childhood. If I wasn't drawing then I was writing poems.

Nine years ago I left my husband, my three children, a brand new house, furniture we had just bought, a boat, cycles, etc. It was like I did not think I was good enough to deserve it all. I had to get out, I did not leave him for someone else. It was like letting a caged animal loose. I went out almost every night, screwed everyone I met. I even tried prostitution.

After some time my daughter moved in with me; the boys stayed with their dad. She's been with me for about five years; she'll be 17 next month. She has slowed me down a lot. My husband and I got a divorce, and neither one of us has remarried. I met a man six years ago; he takes care of me sexually. He's older than me and he has the softest hands. Yes, he satisfies me and I'm his woman. Sexually I can cope with him, otherwise I can't; that's why we are not married.

I'm still trying to find and understand the way I am. I have never thought much of myself. I have never had much self-esteem, self-worth, and self-image.

I still have so much self-hate in me. I have been off and on anti-depressants half my life.

My aunt and uncle died years ago. I hate him now. I hate him for ruining my life, depriving me of my childhood. He took my life and soul and played with it like a toy. Didn't he know how much it would affect me when I got older?

My younger sister (38) and I have never talked about it, but we will one day. She is like me, she talks a lot about sex, and she has always been sexually active. My older sister (41) and I sat down a few years ago and talked about it. She said she hated what our uncle did. We never told anyone, not our parents, no one.

Last month a girl and I went out drinking one night. She told me how her father had abused her and I told her about my uncle. We both talked and cried together. I have never had counseling; I looked into it once but it cost too much money so I never did. Maybe someday I will. I still have so much buried inside of me.

Nancy Lee

PROGRESS REPORT ON NANCY LEE

The past couple of years I have been seeing a psychologist. We have had long talks about the past and I think talking about it with a professional really helps. A person shouldn't keep everything inside, they need to let it out and talk about what happened to them, even though it hurts. I hope everyone realizes how important therapy is, and how much it really helps.

My sister and I now have talks about our abuse. She did something I never could do. She sat down with our mom and told her about the sexual abuse with our uncle. She said it was like a heavy load was lifted off her shoulders, because I was the only one she had ever talked about it with.

I still have blocked out a lot of what happened back then, and I sometimes think it is buried so deep it will never come out. But, I am doing better. I have a boyfriend now; it's been ten years since my divorce, so each time I meet someone I think maybe this will be the one.

PANDORA'S BOX

Pandora's box locked
away for many, many years
Hidden secrets of days
to be forgotten.

Brought to life,
so that yesterday
begins to feel like today.
Panic begins to take control.

Losing ground quickly
the battle continues
fighting to gain a footing
only to be swallowed up
by a flood of unknown emotions.

Afraid, confused, and
misunderstanding all that
has gone on before, so scared
of what is to come.

Now shared with a chosen one
who can help
dispel the load of pain.
The burden is somewhat lifted.

Crystal Ann Jordan

PROGRESS REPORT ON CRYSTAL ANN

My recovery process continues day by day, minute by minute. When I wrote my poems I was only beginning to understand what long-lasting effects the abuse had on me.

With the help of a supportive therapist, who keeps me honest with myself and pushes me towards further growth, I have begun the process of reparenting myself. I am growing up all over again. Admitting the abuse, dealing with my own strong denial system, accepting the hurt, anger, and disappointment have all been steps in my therapeutic journey.

Perhaps the most important thing for me to do was to establish a healthy support system, with loving, nurturing men and women who care about who I am as a person. Finding a best friend for the first time in my life has been richly rewarding. Abby and I realize our own limitations and understand each other for who we are. I thank her for teaching me that lifelong lesson.

I am actively pursuing my newly established long- and short-term life goals. This includes obtaining an M.S.W. so that I can help other victims. Exploring and expressing my emotional self through art, music and writing has been helpful in dispelling the long- term depression I fight on a daily basis. Learning to control and accept my emotions and not let them control me has perhaps been the hardest task.

I have recommitted myself to God, and am active at my church in working with children and singing in the choir. Finally, I have forgiven my molester and those who allowed it to happen.

SPEAKING

i went to a conference today
on sexual abuse
only i was not learning
i was living.

i felt creepy because
i was the topic
labeling is creepy

there were perpetrators there
and victims
i could feel it

i did a panel discussion
and the mental health professional said
i had courage

i said no
this is my day
of revenge

i guess that is
courage
considering
step
by
step

Cecilia

REVULSION

my mouth feels like a catbox

a catbox with slime in it —

probably because it has a penis in it.

i do not want a penis in my mouth.

then why is it there?

no one cares anyway.

my mouth will probably always feel like a catbox

with slime in it.

no one cares anyway —

but the cat who wants to get in.

Cecilia

SURPRISE

i said

if i told

my father would never speak to me.

my mother would have a nervous breakdown.

my oldest brothers would have marital problems.

my perpetrator brothers would be exposed and get sick.

their perpetrator friends would deny — and then laugh.

my sister would hate the chaos and gain weight — all the while denying.

my youngest brothers would not understand — but they really would.

sexual abuse runs in families you know — a filthy epidemic.

society would point their fingers.

i sure do have a lot of power.

the world sure does revolve around me.

well nothing much happened

the world continued to spin on its axis

everyone denied

and

i

got

healthier.

Cecilia

MY BROTHER

My brother lives in a box of cigars.
Each day every day
he lifts the lid to peek at the world
and hopes the world won't notice.
Bristles grow on his face and throat.
He smells, fears soap.
He never throws his loose hairs away
but carefully keeps them, dirty and dark,
in the teeth of his green plastic comb.
Long ago he spent years committing incest.
I survived but we never mention it.
He's 35 now and still lives with our mother.
My favorite joke when I visit is to talk
of the time I stabbed his thigh with a fork
and sent him screeching around the table
for ruining my first perfect crayoned picture.
We pretend to laugh and the scar
does not go away. Migraine headaches
take me back to the fork, to the fort
he built under cool pines
where he wouldn't let me visit
unless I would and I did.
Now he does his best to repel.
He rots his teeth, sucks his cigars,
growls and belches and gets fat.
Each night every night
he grows a little smaller inside.
One morning my mother, weeping,

may find he's flickered out at last,
a tiny gray heap in an ash tray.
I'll visit, leave the jokes behind,
bring instead a perfect crayoned picture
to wrap around his coffin.

Blanche Woodbury

PROGRESS REPORT ON BLANCHE

Through the writing of poems about my experience of incest with my brother, I was able to bring myself to talk about it with people close to me. In fact, the public reading of this poem was my way of finally telling my best-friend-since-age-ten Rose, who was in the audience; then I was able to talk with her directly.

I began a teaching position which has provided me with enough income and benefits to enter weekly therapy with the express goal of working on the effects of my incest experiences.

After a silence of 25 years, I approached my brother and we talked about our past! That initial conversation lasted only 20 minutes or so, but it was one of the most significant acts in my life. This is partly because it enabled our dying mother to know that we would now try to continue as a family even without her as the link between us, which had been one of her roles due to his and my mutual estrangement.

What I have to say to others who have experienced the feeling of damnation due to being an incest victim is this: Write honestly what you know in your heart is true and then dare to speak it out with as much compassion — for yourself as well as for those who caused your pain — as you can muster. No one can make you feel ashamed if you don't let him or her. Call on your anger and use it to heal instead of hurt.

NOT INCEST

My sister cried not incest
My mother cried in rage not incest
I took Xanax and yodeled and my knuckles
went white saying, not incest, not rage
One universal voice said Don't speak I
went tight saying no bad words Odious,
Queer thoughts formed in my head till I
went deaf on the great taboo, went blind
and tight and white saying not incest

Sandra Joel Ahrens

INSIGHTS AND PERCEPTIONS

A tremendous burden is placed upon a child when there is so much pain and nowhere to go with it. It often gets sealed up in a box and buried. Nobody sees the lingering scars.

Keeping distressing secrets for a long time denies you the opportunity to be whole. It restricts your freedom to be you, because you are not quite sure who you really are. A part of you seems to be missing. This chapter shows some of the resulting loneliness and isolation we experience from others and even within ourselves.

It is important to begin to open the box and carefully let out some of these secrets. This is a very scary thing to do, especially if you don't know what is there. As the feelings come, it may seem as if you are losing ground and being overwhelmed by a flood of hidden emotions. Make sure you have a support network and begin to trust them and yourself, knowing you are in control and stronger than what is locked away. Enter slowly into the dark and carry your inner light with you.

BE BRAVE

CHAPTER FOUR

LOVE THAT HURTS

"I want to scream because his way of loving me was to use me."

Crystal Ann Jordan

UNINVITED

Time now is a challenge as you are portrayed in my mind

The childhood dream a young girl has

was never really mine

You scarred my life, my dreams, my time.

It was not yours to interfere.

You sliced right through and created,

Your own life in my years.

Beth LaMontagne

WARPED ALLIANCES

My life
Has been filled
With
Warped alliances
Obsessions about
Your reactions, your needs,
Your feelings, your wants,
Your perceptions, your desires.
Not that it is
Wrong
To care
For you
But it is
Deadly
To care less
For
Me.
See
What
I
Mean?
Warped Alliances.

Rylee Brown

I Want To Scream

I want to scream because I was so little when
    he ripped my soul out of me.
I want to scream because I was so little when
    he choked me and hit me and fondled me.
I want to scream because I was a woman before
    I was a child.
I want to scream because his way of loving me was
    to use me.
I want to scream because he molested me in the starkness
    of the day and not just in the shrouded night.
I want to scream because I cannot pretend
    he was a monster under my bed.
I want to scream because I was so little.
    I want to scream because he didn't protect me.
I want to scream because he thinks I made it all up.
    I want to scream because of so many years of pain.
I want to scream because of the times — over and over
    that I hurt myself, tried to kill myself
because the pain was so great.
    I want to scream because of all the hurt I have caused
others when I unleashed my pain on them.
    I want to scream because I have no parents.
I want to scream because the struggle to find my voice
    has been so long and cost so much.
I want to scream because I was born beautiful, with a spirit and
    a voice and all of this was methodically tortured
out of me by people who said they loved me.

alyssum

HISTORY

The earliest memory of family terror I have is when I was two years old. Grandma was babysitting me and my brothers, ages four and six. All three of us were in our pajamas and playing in the back bedroom of our house. M., my oldest brother, left the room for the bathroom, directly across the hall. When he returned from the bathroom, M.'s hands were held in front of the crotch of his grey and navy, diamond-patterned ski pajamas. He stopped in the bedroom doorway, grinning maliciously at his startled brother and me.

"If the two of you don't do as I say, I'll pee on you!" He appeared to be gripping his penis and waved it menacingly at each of us as he spoke. Having succeeded in terrifying us, he laughed viciously and raised his hands away from his body revealing that it had been an illusion. I stood across the room feeling frightened and powerless while P. gave in to curiosity and asked M. to show him how to create the illusion.

Complaining to Grandma about M.'s terror tactics would have been futile since he was her favorite and he had already learned that complaints about him could be effectively dealt with by accusing his victims and saying, "They're crazy. They don't know what they're talking about!"

✦ ✦ ✦ ✦

On my way home from school one Halloween afternoon, a stranger called me over to his car under the guise of looking for an address in the area. When I looked through the car window, he was jerking off. I was fascinated but the situation felt unsafe. I referred him to the school for directions and talked my way out of danger by telling him that I had to get home before my father came looking for me.

He drove away and I walked home desperately needing to feel safe, and found my mother angrily shoveling shingles out of the driveway. Somehow I knew that she wasn't available to me so I buried the incident in silence. After that I noticed that my mother was always too busy, preoccupied or angry to be available to me.

✦ ✦ ✦ ✦

Grandpa's sisters lived in California so when he and his second wife came to visit, they stayed at our house between making the rounds of his sisters' homes. They came to visit the winter I was in fifth grade. Grandpa's green and white Cadillac was parked in our garage and I was helping him pack the car for a trip to one of his sisters'. I was wearing flannel pajamas under an ankle-length corduroy bathrobe. When we started back into the house, Grandpa grabbed me from behind and forcibly held me against him while he repeatedly humped against my backside. Once again I managed to act externally calm and controlled in order to talk myself out of a dangerous situation. Until he died I remained quiet about the incident, knowing that my mother was devoid of the resolve to banish her father from her house, if she believed me. I doubted that she would believe me.

◆ ◆ ◆ ◆

With the onset of puberty my parents felt a joint obligation to inform me of the biological changes I would experience as a part of becoming a woman. At bedtime one evening, my father came into the room, sat down on the side of the bed, and delivered an emotionless and vulgar speech about the woman's body that would be mine. During a reference to breast development he told me: "If your tits itch and hurt as they develop, it's part of the normal process." To this day when men refer to women's breasts as "tits" I have the urge to throttle them for their vulgarity.

Later, in adolescence a couple of dark hairs had sprouted from the edges of my nipples. Mother came into the bathroom while I was drying off after a bath, plucked the hairs from my breasts and declared, "We don't want hair growing there, do we?" I felt violated and angry that having three hairs growing from my chest made me a failure as a woman.

◆ ◆ ◆ ◆

Things continued to be cyclically violent, with violence and the blame directed at me. To escape such a volatile environment, I attempted suicide with an overdose of Thorazine. I failed and had that humiliation added to my failure. The repeated visits to the psychiatric emergency room, coupled with the suicide attempt, despite weekly therapy, resulted in my admission to the long-term adolescent psychiatric ward.

During my hospital stay I didn't have the perspective to describe my family as dysfunctional. I thought all kids got beat by adults. The professional staff lacked the expertise to recognize the symptoms. When the time came for my release, I couldn't communicate why I was terrified of returning home, so I attempted another Thorazine overdose and almost succeeded.

✦ ✦ ✦ ✦

On Saturday mornings, while I sat in bed reading, M. would come into my room and get into bed with me. He would trap me in a corner and fondle my breasts through my shirt. When I asked him what he was doing he answered, "Loving you!" This happened repeatedly and resurrected my dread of weekends.

Over breakfast one Saturday, after he had forced his way into my bed again, I announced to our parents, "Tell M. that if he wants to cop a feel to go buy himself a whore and leave me alone!" In response to parental silence, M. smiled arrogantly and answered, "She's crazy. She doesn't know what she is talking about. After all, she was the one who was locked away!" The subject was dropped since it was easier to believe that I was crazy than to admit that the entire family was fucked up. I knew that my "home" would never be a safe place for me.

✦ ✦ ✦ ✦

Dad had his moments of unreasonable violence, usually when he was drinking, but Mom was an expert at dispensing horror with no apparent reason or cause. I remember the coldness of the tile bathroom floor through the bath-mat I was made to lie on while mother administered enemas to me. In contrast to the cold floor was the scalding tap water that she poured over my pubic area. Ask her about the slappings, enemas or the scalding tap water and she'd deny them all and claim that I imagined each of these horrors.

✦ ✦ ✦ ✦

I started attending workshops provided by Prevention Services at a local women's alcohol recovery program. Through the workshops, my reality has been validated by the other participants. I also see a therapist while I work through the issues of surviving my victimization.

I will continue to speak about my experiences, no matter who denies or tries to manipulate my reality. I still have a lot of work to do before I can say I have overcome my own tendencies towards violence and can feel safe in sexual situations. I'm also working to acquire the social skills that being socially isolated deprived me of. I stay away from those social situations, family gatherings, that my instincts tell me are threatening or unsafe for me.

I am angry that getting healthy is such a long process and that I was denied a healthy, loving, nurturing childhood. I now do what I can to make the world a better place for myself and the next generation.

S.M.

PROGRESS REPORT ON S.M.

Two years ago, I became homeless as a result of a long-term physical illness. Fortunately, I have kept a roof over my head by exploiting the shelter system and various friends. A sense of adventure has been essential to surviving relocation every 14 to 60 days.

To continue my process of healing, I am surrounding myself with supportive people who trust me to know what I need in order to heal physically, mentally, and spiritually. Hopefully, I have a sense of adventure about my healing process similar to that which has helped me to survive being homeless. Creativity, tenacity, humor, and a sense of fascination can heal most any trauma and convert scars to badges of triumph.

I still have a lot of unresolved, unexplored areas related to being abused. I am in no hurry now that I can control how fast or well the healing process works. I'm getting better at trusting my sense of what feels safe. I also periodically do a 12–step program.

INNOCENCE

it starts when you're a little girl
long before puberty
with crinolines
under dresses short enough to show
four-year-old thighs
and all the women say,
"How pretty!"
the men sit you
on their knees and touch
the pink tops of your legs
with sandpapery fingers
and pat your cotton panties when you rise
you're a princess, you're an angel
you're a beauty with fine legs
and wide eyes
it continues when you get too big for laps
advances through cheek pinching
and graduates to ass slaps
and how to act like a lady lessons
your Mom provides
the men admire you with guilty eyes
that lead you to notice Aunt Mary
frowning at Uncle Joe
you're learning that men are animals
what everybody knows
it's important to please them,
the tacit assumption goes
you become a fallen angel

temptation in a body that bleeds
as it grows
you carry stains on your clothes
but wear a mask of purity
for show

Roseanne O'Brien

PROGRESS REPORT ON ROSEANNE

I can only say that what changed my life from a cycle of failure and pain and a self-defeating inner program was my decision to take responsibility for one task and to see it through. That task was going back to college. I focused myself exclusively on earning my degree. Relationships with others took a back seat. I lived alone and I worked hard. I graduated as a different person, and that is when I began. No longer timid, I earned my self-confidence. I knew I could achieve something on my own, and I had created a new identity. The past lost its hold over me.

Today, I am happy in my marriage, and I enjoy being the kind of parent for my own daughter that I never had. This is my ongoing healing. I work as a probation officer, and I deal with sex offenders on a regular basis. I believe I can do a more effective job because I know from my own experience what sexual abuse is really about.

At times, I felt like a toy that he would take down from his shelf, play with for a while, and then put away. I came between his interest in toy tugboats and his thrill of getting his first car.

Anonymous

I'LL NEVER TELL

I'll never tell . . . a secret of yours
If you did it or didn't do it
So . . . trust me . . .
Care for me . . . and be a friend
That's all I'll ask of thee.

✦ ✦ ✦ ✦

DEAR RAIN

Rain coming down
Like tears in the sky
If there is love for me
Like there is rain
Why doesn't anyone
Care for me.

✦ ✦ ✦ ✦

I REMEMBER

I remember . . .
When that cruel hand struck
I remember . . .
When that leg kicked up
I remember . . .
Cuts and bruises
I remember . . .
My parent's abuses.

Tiffany
Age 12

VIRGIN POEM

If we lived in the South Sea, long ago,
brother, you might have been husband
or lover taking me in the flowered tent
in ritual, at the festival.
My friends would have brought me shells
and coral, combed my fine brown hair
back from my face, giggling
to think of kisses there. To think
of you, older brother, striding into the tent
to find me there on the sweet soft cloth
stretched upon the sand, my breasts
years from blossom, my hips
straight and narrow as a young palm.
Oh, your manroot there. Your hands
tender and gentle with knowledge
taught to you by the village fathers,
tradition, protecting me from evil
spirits that would gather to my hymen.
You would hurt me, yes, but you
would recognize my pain, acknowledge
tears, go on loving me as clean
little sister, and I would know
the pain would end and leave me whole.
How different, brother, in this northern land
where you tore my flesh and left me broken,
dirty secret, shameful sister
knowing eight years into life
love is a jagged island of ice
where flowers never grow.

Blanche Woodbury

HEY YOU

I wrote *Hey You* on Friday night after work, after first cancelling my plans to go out with a friend, as I felt too depressed and fatigued to be with anyone. I felt an unexplained sense of impending doom, terrible isolation and confusion as I took off my nurse's uniform to take a warm bath and to attempt to relax a little. My sense that something bad was about to happen persisted through the bath as did the badgering voice inside my head saying . . . why do you have to be depressed all the time, what's the matter with you anyway, always thinking of yourself, never thinking of anyone else, grow up, etc. etc. Words I learned from my mother at a very early age.

I've had enough therapy and have enough health to know that when I'm feeling this low, it's really important to intervene on my own behalf, before I sink even lower. My incest group leader had mentioned in group the night before that I might want to write a letter to my father, as I had been struggling with a lot of unanswered questions about his abuse of me. I knew he had sexually abused me many times, but could only clearly remember one particular incident. So I decided to start a note to him this Friday night.

Within one hour my *Hey You* letter came out through what I call automatic writing. It isn't truly automatic, but the words pour out without censorship, and with each word comes an enormous sense of power. The power I never had as a child becomes mine as words and fury hit the paper. I write to exhaustion and then read what is before me. And with the reading and re-reading comes a sense of relief to have so much bad stuff outside of me and to see this bad stuff for what it really is. Not an ugliness that is me, but a badness that was done to me.

This particular piece was healing for me, as I had never before been able to express any anger at all toward my father. He was a sick man, he was an alcoholic, he couldn't help it, he suffered so much throughout his life . . . But my father committed some really heinous crimes against me and my two siblings and I feel it is important for me to look at them now and work through the pain, so I can become the best me possible. Perhaps then, any goodness I might have would counteract his evil.

Hey You!

That's right, I'm talking to you. I won't call you Dad or Father or Daddy or Joe or Joseph. You are nothing more than a Hey You and you don't even deserve that much courtesy. You deserve to be beaten and tortured and humiliated in prison where no one calls you by name, where things are done to you without salutation, where syphilitic homosexuals come up to you from behind. Then thugs, that's right, hey you, big mean fat nasty thugs who use brass knuckles to punch your fat belly so hard and so repeatedly that you double over, cry out in pain. I hate you, Hey You. I hate you. I want you back here on this earth. Death is too good for you. I hate you and I can't find enough bad words to explain you.

You hurt me, nameless. You hurt me more than you were hurt in my imaginative pay-you-back prison. You used me. I was nothing to you but a toy, not even a treasure toy. I was your disposable, breakable ten-cent toy. You bought me for cheap. You used me and disposed of me and repurchased me time and time again. Your dimes came out as fast as the click, click, click of an ice cream man's silver belt-changer. Dimes at the flick of a finger. Dimes to buy JoAnnie, breakable, throw-away baby doll.

Did you know me, nameless? Did you ever wonder who the hell I was? Could you never see the flame of my intelligence behind my provocative child eyes? You seduced me. You stole my innocence. You jobless, worthless, "un-man" — man. I had nothing but abstracts as your child. Abstracts like purity, cleanliness and innocence. You punctured my purity with your blade, leaving me with more abstracts like pain and shame and desperation.

You summoned me with a "let's go" toss of your head. I responded like a co–conspirator, a really small and earnest cooperator. I wanted your love. We'd go someplace together, you remember where, and you would drip my name like honeyed sex juice down your engorged and trembling lip, "Baby doll, come here to Daddy." How dare you call yourself that name! You are a nameless. You are abstract, like the fetid black air seeping from your humid dark grave.

You scared me, nameless. I shake now as I write to you. Where did you take me? Where did we go? What did you do to me? Why do I tremble now? Why am I compelled to write this? Anger has quieted down and in its place is fear. I've been thinking a lot about all the evidence, nameless. My night terrors, calling out, "No, no, no, please help me. I'm going to die," each night in my sleep, in my 39th year, I cry out to someone, "Oh dear God, please help me." There is too much evidence against you, nameless. Two therapists finding puzzle pieces to fit the rape puzzle, the father-daughter-did-it-together puzzle, the JoAnn has blocked out terrifying memories puzzle. You know the answer, nameless. You were there and you were drunk. You hurt me so badly I blacked out. I remember forgetting. Was it the couch, you slippery dick of a man? Your slimy tongue in my mouth, your whale of a body pumping away on me, pressing out my held breath with each clumsy thrust and pump. Each bump and pump pushing me further and further away from consciousness. Each breath out lowering me deeper and deeper into the bloody abyss.

I am remembering.

JoAnn

PROGRESS REPORT ON JOANN

I am doing much better, especially since I became involved with 12-step programs at Adult Children of Alcoholics and Al-Anon. Working with my spirituality has also turned my life around. The most important step I have taken towards my recovery is to establish a relationship with my own inner child.

I didn't really believe that little girl still lived within me until I found a survivors' group where it was safe to feel and share the outrage, fear, shame, guilt, and sorrow. In this group we used big bats to beat pillows which symbolized our perpetrators. This allowed me to cry and let out all those feelings which were hurting me, and no one else. The grief process could then begin to take the place of the depression.

Whenever I'm feeling really badly and I don't know why, I write to my inner child, little JoAnn, and she writes back. She knows the truth. She knows what is going on even when this grown-up is confused. She really likes to play. She is still afraid of a lot of things though. When she is afraid, she gets a lot of comfort from me. She didn't get that then, but she can get it now and she deserves it.

INSIGHTS AND PERCEPTIONS

There is a shock and an ultimate sense of betrayal when you realize that what happened to you was not supposed to happen at all. You come face to face with the lie that has tricked you into believing the abuse was okay, that has allowed the molester to remain alive within you.

With the realization of this betrayal comes a deep sense of loss and confusion. Fantasies of your "wonderful family" and "wonderful life" can no longer be preserved. You begin to doubt yourself when your insides tell you something does not feel right and the reality does not match. Not only is there betrayal from the molester, but also from the world.

This chapter brings up a lot of old unanswered questions about your own reality, about what was and was not okay. Perhaps it is time to challenge what happened and how life was meant to be. Checking that out with someone you trust to be grounded in that truth may be valuable for you now. It is cleansing to be angry, and then to mourn the loss of what should have been and was not.

BE GENUINE

CLINGING TO THE EDGE

"... old memories continue to plague the here and now ... The feeling of losing control comes over me. I find it very hard to keep myself together, when I am falling apart."

Crystal Ann Jordan

JANN'S STORY

The Portland, Oregon, career woman and mother was in her late thirties, frustrated by a lifetime of feelings she didn't understand.

Sometimes she awakened abruptly in the night, petrified that a man lurked in the darkness outside her doorway.

She'd lock the bathroom door — even when she was home alone — and hurry through the closed-eye routine of shampooing her hair, one ear cocked for sounds.

Her shockingly sexual talk and often flamboyant dress attracted male attention; yet she held men in disdain.

And often in a public restroom, as she gazed down at the grungy tile floor, an unexplainable panic would seize her. A childish bargain replayed itself: "I'd lick this floor if ... "

She had become a mystery to herself.

It was time to trace her anxieties and eradicate them from her life. With fear and embarrassment shored up by determination, she began attending meetings of Adults Molested as Children, until week by week the pieces of the painful puzzle fell into place.

As she had suspected, the feelings had their root in "Uncle Vern," her grandfather's brother and her favorite relative. With his distinguished silver hair and adventurous job in far-off Guam, he seemed the epitome of excitement. She thrived on his attention and exotic gifts during his visits home, where he stayed with his ex-wife and their grown daughter, both nurses.

The summer she turned eight, she went to visit Uncle Vern. She had his undivided attention in the big house that was empty all day — a novelty for the oldest of five children. The first day there he promised her some longed-for roller skates, which, at five dollars, her parents could not afford.

The price proved far dearer.

Although none of the rest of his family was a hugger, Uncle Vern was. The little girl liked that — she'd always wished her Daddy was the kind who'd hold his children on his lap. She sat on Uncle Vern's lap a lot. He was a grown-up who thought she was worth spending time with and she felt good.

It wasn't long before Uncle Vern was doing more than hugging. He strayed into her panties and he rubbed her flat little chest.

At night he would tuck her into bed, and she dreaded that. When her two younger sisters visited one night, the eight-year-old protectively slept on the outside of the double bed so Uncle Vern wouldn't touch them too.

It felt good but it also felt bad. She wanted him to stop. She wanted to tell her Aunt and grown cousin, but she sensed it was something they didn't want to hear, and he made her feel as if it was their own little secret. Surely she was just as bad as he was. And she really wanted those skates.

The day they went downtown to buy them, she saw a policeman directing traffic. She wanted to tell him to make Uncle Vern stop the things he was doing, but the policeman was in the middle of the intersection. In the store she headed for the restroom, where she thought about running away. But Uncle Vern waited by the door, and the window was far too high for her to climb out. She'd lick this filthy ol' floor if only she could get away . . .

On her new skates, the girl escaped as often as she could. She whooshed down hills and the breeze made her clean again; the hollow thrump-thrump-thrump of the cracked old sidewalk drummed his words from her ears.

A family picnic ended her visit, and while she caught crawdads with the other youth she looked at all the chattering adults and wondered what they would say if they knew what Uncle Vern was really like. Even with the family bundled into the car and the motor running, he took her on his lap inside the house one more time.

It took the little girl quite a while to get up the nerve to tell her mother what happened. Years later, in the group, she would discover that being able to tell was a rare thing — as was being believed.

The little girl and her family never saw Uncle Vern after that. When he died several years later, she was glad.

But she was 40 before she could begin to bury him.

Jann Mitchell

PROGRESS REPORT ON JANN

What I have done is learn to create personal boundaries. We're born with them; I simply never exercised them. I am doing this through attendance at and reading about Adult Children of Alcoholics and People Who Love Too Much groups and material.

I am learning how to express my feelings instead of pleasing everyone else. I'm learning how to say "no" — something I would never say to my abusive uncle or authoritarian father. I am learning to love myself as I have loved others — a long, painful procedure, but vital for my recovery.

RESCUE

Mellow music, soothes away rough emotions,
   but only for a moment.
Food, tries to cover up the gnawing pain deep
   within my heart, but fails.
Cold, numb, and empty feelings flow through
   my mind, body, and soul.
While strains of self-destruction carry in
   my emotions of daily living.
Clinging to the edge of Life, I struggle to
   reach the safety line.

Crystal Ann Jordan

AN ESCAPE

I feel like there is something I have to write down. It is about music. It is about Neil Diamond. In 1982 I married, and there was horrible stuff, and I ended up in a divorce. I remember I felt so trapped. My husband had taken away my driving privileges so I had to go everywhere with him. I could not use the phone without his permission. We lived in an 8' x 26' trailer with one door and the windows were covered with foil. He kept me locked in and wouldn't let me go outside.

During the day he made me stay in a small office and didn't allow me to talk to anyone except his parents. My life was one beating after another and it kept getting worse. He peed in my mouth and he shaved my pubic hair. When I was pregnant I had to have oral sex with him, until I threw up. One time I got the keys and tried to leave. He ran me off the road with another car.

I felt so trapped. I remember sitting behind the stereo and listening on the headphones to Swan Lake and Neil Diamond records. I'd shut my eyes and pray and dream of the day when I'd escape. In the meantime even though I couldn't physically be free, my mind would escape when I listened to the music. That is how I kept my sanity. I am enormously thankful for Neil Diamond's soft, gentle music because it helped me to cope and gave me the courage to escape a horribly violent world.

P. Finigan

CHILD

My hand is stiff against the metal the car door gripping the handle I can get out I can I'll open the door if she starts she'll have to stop then we're not going far I feel sick in my stomach to be alone with her she'll start she's just chatting her face is tight.

"I got a letter from Anne Tupper, you remember, Rickie Tickie Tupper's mum. Remember in Warwick and we were so poor and you ate spinach from the garden breakfast, lunch, and dinner, and Dad was off working in Birmingham all week. Remember? In the garden, the paddling pool, you played with Rickie Tickie Tupper in the nude and all the people in the building were so shocked. So silly. 'Mrs. N.,' they would say, 'it's not right.' You looked so sweet together and we'd say how you were going to get married."

"Mum, I was two."

"Your childhood sweetheart. He's going to be a lawyer. You were such a happy child."

I look out of the window it's dark I can't see I feel sick I can smell black and sulphur a coal fire must have been Warwick the only place we had one she's going to start I know she is "You were such a happy child. Where did I go wrong? You act as if you hate me. It's that woman. I can't help it, it makes me want to vomit."

She is crying I can tell by the sniffing I watch my fingers and wonder when I'll spring the lock.

"She's sick. A married woman. It must be her change of life. She has four children. You're 14. For God's sake, what do you think she's doing? I went to see a psychiatrist about you. He said it's criminal, she ought to be locked up. He said that. It makes me sick."

I smell spinach and coal I want to spit in her face I think if she touches me I'll vomit she's looking straight ahead tears running down her cheeks my fingers are curling tight I am curling deeper into darkness getting small so small she can't reach me her voice a big belly a wall of flesh enfolding me the doorknob so high above me the door leads to out to down down down cars vroom byebye the vroom vroom greeney gray car dada byebye dada gone water splash water rub towel byebye dada she lies there warm in the bed I crawl in too mama smells different in the bed salty warm mashed potatoes in the bed belly big and warm mama moving   laughing playing castles rocking rocking mama's hands hold tight mama let me go she's breathing funny mama moving me up and down her legs tight around me hairy scratch on my tummy she is crying funny my hands hit on her belly fists on her belly mama let me go inside my head is black and blue screaming in her folds I hate you I hate you my fists sinking in her flesh help help she lies dead she lies still wet slippy fish slippy sweat slippy I cry the hot pee on my leg she pushes me away cold bed sheet cold I cry she cries I crawl she looks at me I know a secret I'm scared what do I know I don't know what she is scared of me she hits me her voice is screaming loud louder her voice dada home dada home dada home he comes home I am scared I hide in the corner and hum she is scared I'll find the words dada dada dada I hum in the corner I don't talk to her dada comes home he tickles me I scream he bounces me on his knee ride a cock horse to Banbury Cross I scream and scream his face changes what's wrong what's wrong with her what's wrong.

I was two two times two is four times two is eight times two is stop it her hands are on the wheel stop her voice climbs inside my head

"What's wrong with you? I am sick of it. Sick of this sulking. I tell you, we're suing her if she ever tries to get in touch with you again."

I make myself look at her her face is blotched and speckled she is gulping air her eyes are swelling her face her body her arms and legs spread out there's nowhere to breathe I'm five foot eight I watch my fingers tighten on the handle then how the door swings open wide and the cold blue air rushes in and she is screaming screaming I can't hear her my feet climb out of the car I don't look around I know she's crying I know I'll have to go home again.

Nina

WRITING TO RECOVERY

I am 30, single, have a Master's degree in counseling and am assistant director of our local mental health clinic. On the inside I am still a very confused second grader who, despite my years of training, education and competence with other recovering victims, have only in the last year entered therapy to recover myself. You know the thinking — "That's okay for everyone else, but once a therapist finds out those things about me, he'll despise me as much as I despise myself."

I could list a hundred and one other reasons I never sought help. Mostly fear. All these years I buried it and until recently never thought of myself as a victim. Of course it was my fault — there had to be something evil or wrong with me or else this person whom I loved and trusted would never have hurt me. I must have deserved it in some way, I thought. I am working on this part still.

I have kept a journal of my therapy, with volumes of pages about recovery, obstacles to recovery, and about the process. I started the journal because I had such a hard time talking, and being a therapist myself I was pretty well defended and resistant. As I read through my entries it often seems like there are two people talking — one who is still trying to make sense out of it all and still loves the offender, and the other person who is so angry and hurt she just wants him dead. As I read what is written I think this certainly isn't the superficially self-confident person I present at work and on the streets. It's frightening that two different people reside in one body. One is so intent on making her position known and the other is afraid and wants peace at all costs, avoids and denies the whole thing. I can see progress in my journals but as Robert Frost says, "Miles to go before I sleep."

My therapist has most of my writings because I didn't want them in my house in case anyone found them or I died and relatives found them — I worry about what they would think about me. It's so funny, you go out of your way to convince people that you are competent, respectable, happy, well adjusted, and yet on the inside you are a total mess of guilt and shame. You worry that if people really knew you they wouldn't accept you. Sounds pretty crazy coming from a person who was listed last week as a "Woman of Achievement."

I have been working on my "therapeutic letter" to the offender, and I've tried three times. The first time I started out all right and ended up apologizing for everything and being scared to death that somehow he would know I told someone and be angry with me. Funny how strong the memories and experiences are that make you feel he has the power to somehow still hurt you.

My second letter was an improvement but is funny now. I wrote about all the ways my life had been affected and changed and how much self-hate and self-defeat I have felt. I wrote about depression and relationship problems I'd had, but again it was written in a way that I guess I still wanted him to care and feel bad about all the trouble he caused. I am learning emotionally, as I already knew intellectually, that sex offenders are manipulative, power-oriented people, who don't care in the least about their victims.

I remember my therapist, not so subtly, suggesting that part of what was hard was that the offender was my first love, that it was hard to accept his not caring, and so it was easier to hate and blame myself than him. Boy, was I furious — I swore I'd never see that quack again. But it was pretty true. I did love him and that's what hurt so very much — that I loved and trusted so much and he violated my trust, my body, and my soul.

At any rate, I finally finished a letter that I can live with. It really did bring relief and a start towards my future. In lots of ways it just pointed out to me the areas I needed to work on. I guess I wonder if I'll ever get over some of those feelings. I have such problems with touching. Sometimes it feels so gross because it reminds me of how ashamed and dirty and disgusted I felt in the past, and the feelings of helplessness. It especially bugged me that my body responded — it's like I felt betrayed by my own body.

I don't know yet how one learns to give and receive affection in a normal relationship. I hope I can learn. I've been numb for so long and avoided anything but friendship with men. I've done some pretty self-destructive things in the past like getting drunk and just picking someone up. I was really in love with a man once but when it came to the commitment I just couldn't do it. I never thought he could accept my past and help me with the sexual problems. I feel very sad about that now because I think he would have understood. Crazy, but somehow I felt so bad about myself that it was hard to believe anyone else could love me.

When I first went to see my therapist (it was April of last year), my goal was to be finished by June. It's been almost a year now and I see the progress, but it seems like I may be at this forever. I hope not. How long does it take people to get "normal"? I guess like I tell my clients, "As long as it takes." I never thought it would be so hard. I still can't talk about what happened and maybe that's not important. It's been very difficult to trust a therapist. As much as I knew intellectually, I couldn't convince myself that he would understand. I do want to put a plug in for women not being afraid to see a male therapist. I have found it to be advantageous in the long run.

In spite of how long the road ahead is, I am making progress. I can see I'm changing and for once in a long, long time I feel hopeful about the future. It may not seem like it but I've come a long way in these past months and years. On vacation, I took some risks and did things I never dreamed I'd feel enough confidence to do. I'm starting to feel like a person and not so very crazy. I'm even starting to feel a little genuine self-respect.

Anonymous

PROGRESS REPORT ON THIS AUTHOR

I recently received a scholarship to law school and am no longer working in the mental health field. Speaking as a former mental health worker, I feel the system of treatment for victims can be incredibly abusive. I am a survivor, in spite of what happened to me, and in spite of the system of therapeutic "helpers." I will be a successful attorney! Maybe someday all this will come together and I will have a successful personal life to go with my professional life. Work has always been my escape, and something I do well.

When I started writing, I only remembered bits and pieces of my past. I was plagued by horrible nightmares. Through the work I started with my last therapist, I remembered most of it. As bad as it was and as much as I wanted to forget it and excuse it away, I know I am getting better because the nightmares are gone. I guess there is something to be said for confronting the darkness. However, the pain is still very real.

Sharon M. Johnston

Editor's note: We want to caution you that this woman's experiences may be extremely upsetting to read about, and we urge you to follow your own judgment and instinct in deciding whether to read this story. Take care of yourself first and foremost. All the names and locations in this story have been changed to protect the rights of the victims.

Because the following story is extremely powerful, violent and graphic, we have taken the liberty (with the author's permission) to omit some of her experiences. We feel that the reader can grasp the impact and intensity of the abuse from the parts of the story we include below.

We realize that this may be overwhelming and difficult to read but we also want to emphasize that this type of abuse really does happen. If child abuse is going to stop, we have to give society a reason to stop it. Regardless of whether or not this makes the reader uncomfortable, we cannot turn the tragedy of abuse into a fairy tale. The hopeful ending comes from determination, hard work and the guts to come forward and survive the ordeal. We want this story to make a difference.

LAURIE'S STORY

One year has passed since that day in Jim's office when he said, "Laurie, have you ever been sexually abused?"

How did he know? I had tried for years to get someone to hear and believe my story. In 1978 I went to the police to report my father for molesting me but I was swiftly hurried off to a psychiatric facility and was never allowed to talk about what he was doing. I tried to get somebody to help me expose my father but his credentials as a former police officer outweighed anything I had to say.

My mother kept denying the truth even after witnessing my father sexually abusing me when I was six years old. She let him off the hook because she knew he was intoxicated at the time and he swore that he had no knowledge of what he had done. He also reassured her that it would never happen again.

I spent 36 years hiding my father's secrets. Why did Jim ask me if I had been sexually abused? Why should I tell him? After all, he was part of the mental health system where I had spent the past eight years trying to get help for myself. Eight years can be an eternity when you need to expose such a terrible secret.

I didn't even like Jim in the beginning. He was another replacement. At times I felt like a used sweater that was not worn enough to be discarded, just handed down and cast aside to the next therapist. Eight years and four therapists had passed and now Jim took charge of my emotional life. He had the book knowledge but acquired more experience working with "victims" of rape and abuse. He said he saw the "cues." Whatever it was, Jim took a stab at the secrets I kept locked away in my mind.

I cried that day last year and was scared to trust that stocky, sometimes smug character who sat across from me. I didn't like the way he looked at me. I was afraid of him. He was a man. Why should I trust any man after what my father had done to me? Why should I trust Jim when his eyes were so scary? I always felt he was looking through my clothes and raping me with those green piercing eyes.

What I didn't understand, in the beginning, was that Jim looked beyond the barrier I had been shielding myself behind.

In order to trust him I needed to test him. I was afraid to tell him everything at first; I was afraid he would take advantage of me too.

Jim gave me hope that if I worked at it slowly he could free me from the mental closet I felt safe to hide in with all my secrets.

I felt like a school kid. I left Jim's office last year and told my mother that someone asked me if I was ever sexually abused. I was disappointed because she was still denying that this could possibly be true. Was Mom that naive or was she still trying to protect my father? He was dead, so why not listen to my story? Why keep denying that the man was a perverted cop? He wasn't the upstanding citizen that comes with the legend of the men in blue. My dad should have been sent to the electric chair for what he did to me and my little brother. Dad was a child molester hiding behind a badge and uniform. He was the law — so how do you report a cop for abusing his children?

In 1978, nobody would believe that a 30–year–old woman could be molested by her father. What they didn't understand was that it started as a child. A little girl who would grow up someday.

A girl who would bury the secrets but never forget them.

My father ruined my life but since Jim has worked tediously these last 12 months, I have new goals to aim for. I need to talk about the secrets, the scars, the hell of being raised by a child molester. I feel compelled to tell my story so people like my father don't keep destroying innocent children.

The drawback of telling it all is that you give these perverts ideas. My father enjoyed reading everything about criminal behavior. Dad probably got some of his ideas from the criminals he locked away. My mom can now recall that dad would bring home police reports, the macabre stories of sexual crimes, and read them or ask her to read them aloud. Stories about rapists who would kill their victim first and then cut them open and have sexual relations with a vagina ripped out of a body. It was the bizarre that he enjoyed reading, because he was just as bizarre. He was a criminal who wore a policeman's uniform.

The "cues" Jim saw in his office last year can be written on paper so parents can determine if their spouse or some other adult is sexually abusing their children. Teachers, school nurses and parents should feel a child's head for lumps and cuts that go unattended and unexplained. The lumps and cuts are certainly out of sight so the child molester can inflict pain and fright on their victims without ever being discovered.

In the beginning I could never talk about much of the abuse. I had to write it down and give those notebooks to Jim. I was too embarrassed to talk about the bizarre things my father put me through. I had hoped that if I wrote down the facts Jim would read it and forget it. I was wrong because he made me deal with the problems. Jim was supportive and it was his empathy towards me that kept me going this past year.

This is what Jim made me talk about. This is the story he believes and these are the secrets that changed my life forever. I've changed the names in order to protect myself and my brother from any further abuse.

My life started back in January 1948. I was the fourth child of five born to Jerry and Clara. I spent the first years of my childhood growing up outside the United States in a place called Ancon, Canal Zone.

When dad was old enough he joined the Army and was sent to Fort Clayton in the Panama Canal Zone where he later met and married my mother. After getting out of the Army he became a government police officer, keeping peace and enforcing the law in the Canal Zone. To this day, I can't figure what made him the child molester he was.

He was a big man — six feet tall and weighing anywhere from 180 to 200 pounds. He wasn't flab, just solid bulk. He had a mean face but the most frightening features were those piercing brown eyes.

The Panamanians had a nickname for him. They called my father "The Cyclone." They feared him probably more than they ever respected him. I guess everyone admired dad because he didn't fear anybody or anything. It was his reputation for being a tough cop that people knew. He had his kind moments and he had his friends and a wife that admired him. What they didn't know was what he was doing to his little daughter and his little son Larry.

Dad always claimed that Larry and I were burdens and that he could afford three children and not five. He never thought I was his daughter so maybe that's why I was singled out to endure the brunt of his hostility.

Dad hated me and also claimed my real father was a black man, a Jamaican named Ricardo. Even if this had been true it should not have been grounds for abusing me.

Dad's salary enabled both my parents the luxury of hiring a black maid to take care of the household obligations and rearing of the children. One black housekeeper, who was a partner to sexually abusing me, was Marie.

One of the first recollections regarding Marie is that I had to play the lick a maid game. Dad tried to make it a game, but when they locked me in the refrigerator it was a game I didn't want to play. But I never had a choice.

Dad would stick a wire in either my right ear, my rectum or my vagina. If I didn't lick Marie's genitals, he would send voltage enough to shock and hurt me. If I cried, the punishment was to be locked in the refrigerator.

On one occasion while I was forced to play lick a maid, Marie was menstruating. The blood was never there before and as I licked I felt a terrible pain on the right side of my head. My ear was on fire and my father was screaming at me that I hurt Marie. He was screaming that I did it too hard and that I had to be gentle.

I remember that incident because I thought the menstrual blood was my fault. I hated this game of theirs and I hated when they made me do it. There were times I would be put in the refrigerator for not wanting to play lick a maid. At two years old I was scared, so instead I did what they wanted me to.

Uncle Mac was also a policeman, not a relative, but dad insisted that we call him Uncle. He played the game too and I'd have to lick his genitals as well. I was too little to understand why he would get hard. They would say, "Keep licking but don't bite. Be gentle and don't be so rough." I remember being told to kiss his hard penis and as he climaxed I was shocked again and told I did it too hard. Nothing ever pleased them. I was always being screamed at, shocked, or locked away in the refrigerator in the red kitchen.

I didn't know back then that it was sperm that I was tasting but I grew to be repulsed at this hot, salty, sticky stuff. As I grew up some medicines reminded me of the lick a maid game. Alka Seltzer, Barium swallows, along with Maalox were too awful to swallow, so taking medicine kept the game fresh in my mind. Dad probably thought I'd outgrow and forget, but tasting menstrual blood and semen is something I never got out of my mind.

As I grew older I needed reconstructive surgery to my vagina to correct nerves that became exposed. The doctors could never tell me what caused this condition so it leads me to believe that the wire and shock to the vagina created this problem. Marie was from the West Indies and practiced and believed in voodoo. She convinced my father that he could rid me of my evil ways and I could, forever, be in his power.

Dad learned to wash my eyes out with a solution of sperm, urine and feces. He'd fill my rectum with milk, beer, soda, juice — anything he had on hand. He'd yell at me to hold it in and when the pain was too much and I passed it, he would collect it in a little metal potty pan and then force me to drink away my imperfections. I'd gag and choke but I was forced to do as he told me. When he'd finish he'd wash my rectum out with Murphy's oil soap or a diluted bleach mixture.

He'd ejaculate in my food and make me eat or drink his sperm. At times he'd even urinate and make me drink his piss. These weren't games at all — it was my punishment, he said, for being a bastard child.

Dad destroyed everything I ever loved. On one occasion he used an electric drill and pierced a hole through my turtle's back and killed him. He told me to never tell anyone about his secret games. When he thought I might tell my mother, he took an Oriental cooking wok and drilled holes through it and said it could be my head. He said a turtle shell wasn't any stronger than a head so if I didn't want to end up like the turtle, I better not talk.

He got the message across because he'd make me sit holding the wok on my head and he'd beat it with his nightstick yelling, "Understand?" Dad would keep hitting the wok and the ringing in my ears and the screaming made me afraid to tell.

My mom recalls now that he told her the dog bit a hole through the turtle's shell. She never knew he killed my turtle and I was too terrified to tell her.

Uncle Mac slashed the throat of a kitten and also instilled fear into me. He held the kitten in my face and said he'd do the same to Larry, if I ever told anyone about the lick a maid game.

Dad got ideas with dogs and cats too and even had the family pets participate in the sick sexual games. He'd tie me down and spread milk or tuna fish
oil all over me and let the cat lick me. The process was repeated with the family
dog. It didn't feel good and this extension of the lick game made me very
uncomfortable.

Dad would just make me wait until he'd untie me. I had to learn not to cry,
but most of all not to tell anyone what he was doing.

I had a friend named Arturo. He caught my father at the lick game and was
going to tell. From what I remember about Arturo, he was Marie's boyfriend and
he was a bus driver. Arturo was a tall, thin black man who was my friend. I did
like Arturo because he never played sex games with me. He'd bring little sur-
prises for me, mostly candy.

One day he came and I remember dad and Arturo yelling and fighting.
Arturo was saying that dad was sick in the head and he was going to the police
station to tell.

Dad made me go with Arturo to the railroad tracks that led to the jungle
interior. Dad pointed his gun at Arturo while he pumped the little rail car as it
moved along the tracks heading deep into the jungle.

I didn't know what dad was going to do but I knew Arturo and I were both
scared. When we got deep in the jungle, dad made Arturo put a rope around his
neck. Dad hung Arturo from a tree, and was yelling, "Who are you going to tell
now, nigger?" I saw Arturo's eyes bug out, and he started kicking, but that
stopped by the time dad took me back to the rail car.

Dad told me if I ever told anyone, I'd be like Arturo and no one would ever
find me hanging from a tree in the jungle. He said the animals would eat Arturo
up and no one would ever know what happened to him again.

I don't know how many days or weeks went by before my dad took me back
to the interior to remind me what he had done to Arturo. When we got to the
spot where dad had hung him from a tree, all that was left was the top part of
his body. Animals had been eating away at the body. I remember crying and my
dad kept yelling at me to shut up. He said, "If you ever tell anyone about our
secret games, I will do the same thing to you."

Dad cut the body down and threw it on the rail car. I started screaming
because worms were crawling off Arturo and crawling onto me. Back then I
didn't realize the worms were maggots. Dad kept screaming at me.

He took Arturo's upper body back to the station house and reported the incident as a suicide. No one knew what really happened but me. I couldn't tell because I was afraid. I never forgot my friend Arturo and when I grew up, I named a little fuzzy animal after him. Maybe dad thought he got away with the murder, which in a sense he did, but I never forgot what he had done.

Mom has since remembered and told me that dad was the Deputy Coroner as well as station commander at that time. This is probably why it was easy for him to cover up Arturo's murder. I just never forgot my friend who gave me candy and who was going to tell.

Another game was my dad's version of pin the tail on the donkey. Most of the time my eyes were covered with a blindfold and I was tied to a chair with my legs spread. One by one, a grown-up was brought in to use their tongues and make me the donkey. They would be laughing and kidding about how close they could get to a piece of tail on the donkey. They had their tongues all over me. Dad probably thought I was too little to remember that game but the sight of a string of colored porch lights kept the game fresh in my mind.

Dad played another game called Pirate or buck an ear. Sometimes I'd be blindfolded with that game too but other times I could see what the men were doing to me. An occasional hot light meant they were taking pictures of this game too.

I always saw dad getting money, usually a dollar for each ear. I'd be at the police station and I'd be put in a cell with one of the prisoners. The prisoner would wipe his penis all over me and I couldn't scream because I'd have a gag in my mouth. When the penis would get hard the prisoner would ejaculate in one of my ears.

I spent a lot of time at the police station and I don't know if dad got paid extra but there were times I'd be so caked with sticky dried semen that sometimes they'd urinate on me to wash it off.

The click-click game was the scariest of anything dad ever made me do. One time I was playing with a monkey when dad handed me his service revolver. He put the revolver in my hand and said click it at the monkey. I was afraid of the noise of the gun when dad would click it behind my right ear or else my right temple. Sometimes the gun would fire loud when it was near my ear, so I was afraid and I'd cry.

On this particular day he made me click the gun at the monkey's head. A few times it would click but one time the monkey had no head, just blood all over me. When I started to cry, dad made me eat the blood and sit with the monkey in my lap till it got cold and hard.

Dad made me choose one time between Fernando, my dog, and little Larry. Fernando was on my lap and Larry was sitting across from me. Dad was standing behind me, yelling at me to choose. He said, "Whoever is alive after the click-click, I'm going to fuck." I loved Fernando and I loved my baby brother so I got scared. I took the gun and clicked it at my head. Dad kicked the right side of my back and said, "No, you choose Larry or your dog." Every time I'd put the gun to my head, dad would kick me. I was crying when I shot Fernando but I couldn't click the gun at Larry because I remembered what the monkey looked like when I had to eat his blood.

One day Larry said, "I'm going to tell what you do to Laurie." My dad must have been frightened but most of all he wanted to make sure that neither one of us would tell his secrets.

Dad made two hang-man's nooses and put one on me as well as one on Larry's neck. Dad hung us over the bar in the closet and just before Larry stopped breathing, he cut the rope off his neck.

Maybe dad thought I wouldn't remember, but what child molesters have to know is that we don't ever forget. We bury the secrets in our minds and we try to live a normal life. I learned to keep the secrets by writing backwards, writing code, or even hand signs I made up on my own so I'd never forget dad's evil deeds. I never forgot his secret games.

By the time I was six years old we had left Panama behind and moved to Buffalo, New York. My father was no longer a police officer; now he was a security officer for Brinks Armored Cars and then later, he became a security guard at the Ford Stamping Plant.

Most of the secret games stopped but he was still molesting me whenever he got the chance. We were on the way to his school reunion when he molested me in the front seat of the family car, where he was the passenger, and my mother was driving.

Earlier I told you how my mother was convinced he was too intoxicated to know what he was doing and he reassured her nothing like this would ever happen again. What dad forgot to tell mom is that when I was six and Larry was five, he had me tied up while he molested my baby brother. Dad came over to me and said, "Since you love your little brother so much, taste him on my cock."

I was angry and hated him, so when he shoved his erect penis in my face I bit down on it till he screamed and slapped me across the left side of my head. Dad kept slapping me until I blacked out. I remember Larry crying and saying, "I'll do, daddy, I'll do." Larry was a little boy who was man enough to try to help me.

Of course the slaps to my head made me stop biting but one thing changed forever. After that day in the basement, dad was never again to have an erection.

Dad kept me separated from my brothers and sisters and had me sleep in a bed in the basement. I hated thunder and rain storms because I never could hear him making his way through the darkness to molest me while everyone else slept.

I got an idea one night to let my black rabbit, Blackie, out of his cage. I was hoping that dad would fall over him and break his neck. Anything, I thought, I just didn't want to be molested anymore. That night dad was making his usual night walk and as he came through the kitchen and started towards the basement stairs, Blackie jumped and brushed against his genitals. Dad never expected to encounter the rabbit so he started screaming from fright.

Dad's screaming woke my mother so I was glad for at least one night that he couldn't molest me. Dad was angry so he moved Whitey and Blackie's cage out to the garage.

The only other way I could avoid his night walks was to leave my bed and hide out through the night. I spent so much time hiding from my dad that my schoolwork took a slide. I just got by in school and I knew I could have done better if I had been able to sleep in my bed, without being molested by him.

One thing about being molested or even getting someone to believe me was the fact that dad left my hymen intact. He probably felt if I ever saw a doctor when I was little, how could the loss of virginity be explained?

If having a hymen put me in the category of being a virgin, then that's what I was. I was a virgin until I was 18 years old and fell in love.

I never expected to get pregnant. After all, I had gone this long without ever conceiving a child; why then should it be any different? I wanted to get married and have a child; anything to get away from that house and my father.

The father of my daughter left town and ran out on his obligations, but it never stopped me from wanting a baby to raise. I tried to keep my baby but dad had his own ideas in store for the baby I was carrying.

I called it the Pay Day deal. Prior to me getting pregnant, Larry and I took the Air Force entrance exam. Dad wouldn't let me go in the service. Larry was only 17 and he, too, needed dad's signature to join the Air Force and leave home. Dad made me promise that if I'd give him the baby, he'd sign the induction papers for Larry.

Larry needed to get away from the house as much as I did so I agreed to turn over my baby to dad if he'd sign and let Larry join the service. Everyone must have figured dad to be such a caring, expectant grandfather, but I knew what he planned to do with my baby. I had outgrown his secret games and he needed another child to molest. Dad filled me up on Pay Day candy bars and canned peaches during those last six months of my pregnancy. He said he was paying and buying the little peach in my abdomen.

I outwitted that old fool again. After Larry left for his tour of duty in the Air Force, I contacted my lawyer and told him to place my baby up for adoption.

My little girl was born three weeks later and I cried when I signed the adoption papers. I loved that little baby but I couldn't take the chance of keeping her, especially since I knew what dad had planned for her. Seventeen years have gone by and as much as I miss my daughter, I have to confess that it was the best thing for her that I surrendered her for adoption.

It angered dad so much that he finally signed the papers for me to join the service. I was thrilled and left Buffalo behind for an Army base in Alabama.

I didn't stay in the Army because when they discovered I had a child out of wedlock I was discharged. I got an honorable discharge under fraudulent conditions.

There was no way I'd move back home so four months after being discharged from the Army I got an apartment and was married.

When my nine-and-a-half-year marriage dissolved, I had to move back into my parents' home. By this time I was seeing a therapist at a local mental health facility. It was the beginning of a long struggle to make some sense of my life.

When I lived with my parents, mom was working as usual and dad was now drawing disability from work. He chased me from morning 'til afternoon when mom would get home from work.

I kept telling her about what dad was doing but she never wanted to believe this was at all possible. I told my therapist at the time that this was going on but my parents convinced him that I was not telling the truth.

The psychiatrist at the mental health clinic was convinced I was having severe emotional problems so he gave my parents increased medication to keep me under control. The increased medication made me vulnerable to dad's advances. I had no place to hide.

It was a nightmare living in that home. I had no place to go and no way of controlling myself since dad was the one dispensing the medications the psychiatrist prescribed.

Nobody was believing me and I didn't know how to escape. I told a friend who was living in New York City so he came and took me away from their house. Maybe if my life had been different, I could have done more than just survive the situation.

In New York City, the nightmares caught up with me and created problems for my friend Frank and me. I'd wake up screaming and the landlady asked Frank to have me leave. I didn't leave in the ordinary way though. I overdosed on 275 benadril, haldol, and chloral hydrate. I spent two weeks in the Manhattan Veterans psychiatric ward and another six weeks at Mt. Sinai psychiatric facility.

I spent 36 years keeping the truth buried. I survived the abuse and I survived 14 overdose attempts on my life. It's been almost two years but I feel so fortunate to have found a therapist who is truly professional. Jim helped me turn my life around and make new goals to aim for. My therapy sessions have dropped from three times a week to once a week and by the end of next month the doctor will have me off all psychiatric medications.

The days, weeks, and months spent in mental hospitals are behind me now and I look forward to building a new life for myself. All it took was one kind man saying, "I didn't know how serious the abuse was and I believe you"; that unlocked the secrets I had kept buried.

If any of you are having a hard time getting someone to believe your story, just keep talking until somebody listens. Don't be afraid to talk about what happened because it feels so much better to get the truth out.

Anonymous

PROGRESS REPORT ON THIS AUTHOR

Since I wrote this story my therapist Jim was replaced. His replacement left after five months and I now have another therapist. I find the mental health system quite frustrating. If I have to repeat the story of my abuse to every therapist that takes Jim's place, it cannot possibly help me to get on with my life.

I have a whole new batch of problems, because I have been given the house where my father molested me as an adult. This is one of the main reasons I have gotten back into therapy. It has been very hard trying to escape some of the memories that this house holds for me. But I am determined not to let the bad memories of this house get to me or make me think of my childhood.

I have become a born–again Christian and have gotten a lot of help from the Lord and my Christian friends. I know that without them I would be in the hospital. I found helping out at church and getting into bible study helps with my depression. I am surviving because of faith counseling and friends who pray for me but most of all who accept me, an abused little girl that grew up with a lot of scars and pain.

I pray that my faith gets me through the obstacles or nightmares that are ahead of me. I pray too that my story can help people understand that abused children grow up to be adults with a lot of emotional scars. Emotions can be healed but scars never do heal.

INSIGHTS AND PERCEPTIONS

There is a difference between surviving and coping. To us, survival is getting through the actual abuse, while coping is handling it afterwards. "Clinging to the edge" may describe how you feel when trying to cope. People cope in a lot of different ways: 1) thinking that self-destruction might hold something better than life, 2) engaging in self-mutilation to punish themselves rather than expressing the anger, 3) becoming hardened so nothing can hurt them again, or 4) filling their lives with other things to protect themselves from their own intense emotions.

Sometimes it is easier to cope than to deal with your experiences and feelings. This may be because dealing is unfamiliar, while coping is what you learned to do best at an early age. Understand that dealing happens gradually as you channel your energy toward taking care of yourself. Look at what you do to cope with the trauma and see if it is getting you what you really want and need. It is all right to keep the coping skills that lift you up and keep you strong. Discard the habits that continue to hurt you like the abuse did. You are worth pampering, so be good to yourself.

BE GENTILE

CHAPTER SIX

ALONE INSIDE MYSELF

"I cannot crawl outside myself and lose the pain and trauma that pushes at my ribs and threatens to break me and scatter the pieces on the path to nowhere. I am so busy fighting for sanity, whatever that might be, that I have lost contact with my real emotions."

Anonymous

THE LITTLE GIRL

I cannot write on this. I don't know what is not there — except, maybe, The Little Girl. She was not able to live in it so she had to leave and not be. There was no place for her in this world. She got hurt too much to be. She could not stay where there was nothing except pain; and she will not come until she knows that there will not be the pain.

But it is her pain. She will have to go with me. I cannot do the work without her. I will help her. I will hold her. But I cannot do it until she can say it is her pain as well as it is mine. She's the one that lived through it. I did not. I came after. I know it is a lot easier for her to stay where she is than to come and say it hurts. She is the one who hurts. She is the one who cannot laugh. She is the one who cannot tell. She is the one who has to tell what happened. She is the only one who knows.

She is the one who needs to be held. She is the one who needs to hear she is okay even if she is in a 31–year–old body. She still has to come. There is no other way for it. She will have to know that I will take care of her — that I will not let her hurt anymore. I want her to come so that we can become one, so her pain will be mine and my way of not hurting will be hers. Without the two together there will never be one. There'll only be the "Happy-Go-Lucky Verne" and "The Little Girl" who holds the key to the treasure. But to get to the treasure she will have to give me herself. How can I know her treasure without knowing her pain?

Verne

PROGRESS REPORT ON VERNE

What I have done to heal myself is to see a qualified counselor. One who understands the scope of the trauma. I have developed support groups outside of my family. There is not one member of the family that can or will support me in my healing.

Therapy has enabled me to move out of my family home where I have lived for 32 years. I have opened myself up to others. I have a date. Now I have a date to get married. I am even thinking about someday having children of my own.

If I can say one more thing to people who are reading this, and thinking about going and talking to someone, *do it!* It is a lot of hard work, and at times you may even want to quit. But stay in therapy, it is well worth the work. I am still working, though now I can see where the work is taking me. The rewards are unbelievable.

THE WAY IT IS

Light bulbs

and

Razors

and

Pills

Call me by name

"Come use me!"

They beckon me with a

Soft seductive voice

"I will feel good!

I'll give you power!

I'll make you forget!"

I know they are all lies

But sometimes

Lies feel better

Than

The truth.

Rylee Brown

Prostitute's Story

It was midnight. The "witching hour," she thought with an unhappy grin. She climbed out of her second story window into the supporting arms of her favorite tree and slid down the trunk. She crept down the street, silently, and stepped into a waiting car.

Her pimp's name was Rene. At least, that's what he said. She didn't believe anything he said. Anymore.

Tonight he was in a good mood. She knew that meant he had found several well-paying fucks for her. She didn't know how much they paid Rene but she knew what it took to put him in a good mood. Money, and lots of it. Rene asked a higher price for her services because she was so young. She was 13 but only looked 11, if that. Some men wanted to fuck little kids. She didn't care. She knew she'd get what she wanted some day. Soon, she hoped.

Rene dropped her off at his "place." She let herself in the side door and went up to her room. She knew one of those old degenerates would already be waiting for her. That was Rene's style. Let 'em wait. That way they'll be even happier with what they get. She didn't care. She just did what she was told.

She was right. A tubby 60-plus old man was sitting in her rocker. He was nervous. She could tell by how he jumped when she came in and he stopped biting his nails so abruptly. Well, it was her job to relax him. She knew how. She'd done it hundreds of times.

She smiled her brightest smile and snuggled in his soft lap. "Rock me, Gramps," she whispered. "I'm scared. The boogie man is after me." She giggled as he cuddled her. She ran her finger around his ear and began licking behind his ear and along his neck. She talked little girl talk and made appropriate responses but her mind, her real self, was far away. Her body moved mechanically, performing as if this were the first time, as if they were discovering something new in their own secret world, but it was a lie. But what the hell, she thought. He's paying for his fantasy; I'll give him what he wants. She performed for him and for the three gentlemen who came after him that night.

It was when she was with the last john that she let her mind and body come together. She felt a thrill of hope and excitement. Something about this guy told her that she just might get what she had been waiting for. She crossed her fingers and went for it.

While her words and her body performed their very best for him, she kept herself aware in the same room. That was unusual for her but she didn't want to miss anything in this encounter. It was different, somehow.

For one thing, he was younger than most of her customers. He was just about 30, a little bit thin on the top. Black, slick hair, brown eyes. Serious, real serious. If she cared she would have appreciated his hard, lean body, a change from the old flabby ones she usually got. He was slow about getting to it. He'd touch her a little, then stare at her for a long time, then touch her again and then stare again. Touch, stare, touch, stare. If she hadn't had this sense about his being the one to get her what she wanted, she would have been nervous about getting back home before anyone woke up and noticed her absence. But the thrill kept her insides aware and the hope and anticipation made the time spent waiting for his move worthwhile.

Finally, he began to undress her. Slowly. He ran his hands all over her body. Then he began to lick her. She cringed inwardly. She hated the licking more than any other part of doing it, but she made her body move the way he wanted and made the little sounds she knew men paid for. He never said a word and she took his silence as her cue. She put her whole self behind her body into pleasing him. Inside she smiled as he responded to her come—ons, and she prepared herself for the penetration. She felt him grow hard and she exuded a false sense of excitement, pulling at him to come in her. Just as he was about to enter her, he cried out and jumped up. He stared at her wildly and she felt fear mixed with excitement and hope.

As he started towards her again she saw a knife in his hand, and relief mingled with the fear. She was going to get what she wanted after all.

She couldn't help being afraid, but she knew it would be over soon. As he cut into her, he called her a whore and a slut, a slimy bitch, a child of the devil, and through her pain she agreed. He was speaking the truth and he was cutting the evil out of her. She had led a wicked life, but she would die purged of the guilt she had carried for the past ten years.

As he stopped ripping and started stabbing she sank gratefully into the darkness that she had been waiting for, that had been calling to her for so long, and she rested in the deep velvet blackness and died (if only for awhile).

She finally got what she'd wanted.

Janet Wood

DEAR MOTHER

Dear Mother,

You say I can't hold
the fact that my brothers
raped me,
over and over,
against them.

Why not?

Was it right for them
to do this to their little sister?
Did you let them know
it was okay?
Just how blind were you?
How much did you not hear?

Did you ever wonder
why I was afraid at night,
in the day,
of being left alone
with my brothers,
my father,
my cousins?
Did you ever wonder
why I got fat
did a lot of drugs
ran away from home
tried to kill myself
over and over,
mutilated my body
drank too much?

Didn't you ever wonder?

See no evil
Hear no evil
Speak no evil . . .
Just like the monkey.

Blinded by the good life
in lovely Lake Forest Park.
These things don't happen here.

Pamela J.

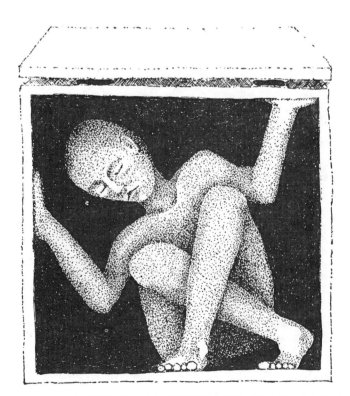

SHADOWS

As I lay on my bed staring at the ceiling, I can't help but feel like I'm all alone, no one to talk to but the restless world.

The restless world, a world I don't want to be a part of, a world that has given me nothing but living hell.

I can see my shadow dancing in the candlelight. She looks so happy, she knows all my secrets, all my wants. She's my only true friend. She's the only living part of me left.

But . . . she's not dancing anymore. The cruel world has swallowed up her zest for life and with her went all my hopes and dreams.

I can see a tear on her cheek as she calls my name, but I can't reach her.

I want this so-called world to give her back to me. They're going to kill her and all I can do is sit back and watch.

Anonymous
Age 15

ODE TO LIFE

Another day of existing without living, of following the lines and signs that give you the appearance of "normalcy," but I know something is different. Though I can escape into a world of robot movements and demands, I cannot crawl outside myself and lose the pain and trauma that pushes at my ribs and threatens to break me and scatter the pieces on the path to nowhere. I am so busy fighting for sanity, whatever that might be, that I have lost contact with my real emotions. I tell myself not to worry, a day will come when I'll understand. And though I let these words spin through me and settle at my feet, I'm still tiptoeing, refusing to get close to myself, my core. If it's there, then so be it. I don't want to know anymore. I don't want to hear or feel or see or speak. I would welcome sensory incapacitation, a blanking out of everything, maybe even breath. Don't misunderstand me, I have no will to die. However, let it be acknowledged, neither have I the will to live. If tomorrow comes, okay. If not, I shall not mourn it as a loss. Nothing can matter that much anymore.

Anonymous

RESPONSIBILITY

The day that I drove away, at 29 years old, I felt so relieved; I had finally escaped. The nightmare was over. I felt so free, so excited, so enthused and eager to start a new life — a life of my own; it was great!

How often do children face adult problems long before they learn to avoid them? How long do they suffer in silence with no one they can trust to talk to? What can a child do anyway? Who will believe them? Why should they have to worry about what would happen to mommy or daddy or whatever adult it is that is abusing them? What will happen to me, my home, my family? How could this person that I admire so much possibly be doing anything wrong?

I was one such child with so much on my mind by the time I was nine years old. I worshipped my step-dad; he was the best and the worst thing that ever happened to me, all at the same time.

When I was six, I was an only child living with my mother and grandparents. I wanted a real family so bad, I was calling my step-dad "Daddy" even before he and my mother were engaged. I was his buddy in no time. He was really a good father. He had raised a lot of other kids by a previous marriage. He was utterly traditional, religious, brave and hard-working. I was so proud of him, and I tried so hard to make him proud of me.

Nothing could have been better for about three years. Then he broke his back for the fourth and final time in a logging accident. I felt so sorry for him and admired his courage so much; it hurt me to see him in such pain.

My mother didn't know how to handle the weight of the burden he had become, and my step-dad didn't know how to handle the fact that she left us for another man.

Looking back on it all now, all that I can think is that something snapped in his mind. I loved him so much as a dad, and I was so confused and ashamed of my mother, that when he reached out in the "grown-up" way I went to comfort him, never realizing what I would have to live through.

After the deed was done, I wouldn't have told anyone even if my mother had been there. I was confused, ashamed, and protective of my step-dad; and I didn't want anything more to happen to him. I didn't know what to do, and he had countless ways to explain that it was all right.

It's not hard to brainwash the young mind of someone who trusts you, especially if you isolate her by managing her life so that she has no close friends. Soon after it all started, my mother came back to us and we all moved out into the country with no phone and no neighbors for miles. The road we lived on was so bad that my step-dad was the only source of transportation. He drove me to school and picked me up right after classes were over. I never got to take part in any extracurricular activities at school, and I was a model student. I never got into any trouble so as not to call attention to myself.

Another ten years of no friends started when he sold the place and bought a motor home. We got to know a lot of country, but no people. By then I felt so responsible that I accepted the responsibility as a lifelong sentence. He had me convinced that if I left him he would die because he loved me and needed me so much. I just couldn't be responsible for letting any harm come to this man I had taken care of for so long. I grew more and more despondent until I just couldn't stand it anymore.

I finally escaped. Now I see the irony of all those years, those wasted years. It bites so hard into the memory of my "childhood" and affects me still for I am the sum total of all those years. It's not easy to live with the irony that the person I believed in and trusted so much used his authority over me to take advantage of that trust.

Even with all the confusion, disgust, and duty that made me grow up far beyond my years, I know that I was one of the "lucky ones." Even so, it almost drove me crazy. I remember that as a teenager I wanted to be as unattractive as possible so I wouldn't have to deal with the conflict that would have developed if I had a boyfriend.

My step-dad was so hypercritical that he had me convinced that it was my moral obligation to stay with him for life. I accepted my fate as a fact of life, and did the best I could with a very unhappy situation.

Looking at my childhood in retrospect, I wish I could have talked with my mother. I was just so afraid. She must have been afraid to face it too. I wish I had just run away.

What I should have done still eludes me. I don't blame myself anymore; I felt like such a fool. My emotions on the subject are still very tender and close to the surface. During the past three years of freedom I have faced these emotions as they surfaced. I am learning to deal with the memory of a domineering man who used a child and ruined a childhood.

Connie W.

INSIGHTS AND PERCEPTIONS

What can you do when the pain is extreme? Where can you go when there is no escape? Whom do you turn to when no one is there? These are tough questions with no easy answers. At the time, escape may seem like the only way to live. Actually it becomes a flight from reality rather than a flight into health. What was intended to protect ends up being destructive. Suicidal ideation, disassociation from yourself, drugs, eating disorders, crime, prostitution, withdrawing from people, and sensory incapacitation are all ways of escaping. None of these are positive or result in healing. They only screen the pain temporarily.

You need to realize you cannot escape from what happened to you or from your feelings. To move toward recovery, you must face and accept all you suffered. It might help to probe through the ways you escape and find what you're running from. Maybe you can call upon others to help you learn new and healthy ways to deal with what is so scary and over-whelming.

Escaping is not living, it is merely existing. You deserve more than that. We encourage you to open your door and find life! Taking another's friendly guiding hand will make it easier.

BE COURAGEOUS

PART TWO

INTO THE LIGHT

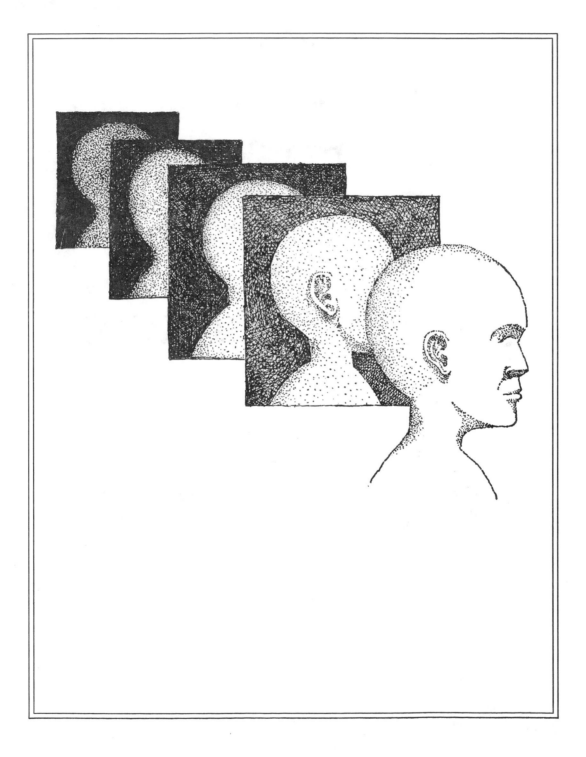

ECHOES FROM THE DARKNESS

"When I remembered nothing it was a problem; not remembering made life impossible.   Remembering is impossible too. Isn't it as difficult to see when there is too much light as it is when there is darkness?"

Suzanne Chamberlin McKnight

TANGLED SCARS

For many years I wondered what was wrong with me. I was always paranoid. I had no friends. I didn't like myself. Then I wondered if it was because I was molested as a child. That was just the beginning . . .

I got married and pregnant at age 18. Everything was fine at first, but after the honeymoon was over our problems began. I couldn't make love to my husband because he had brown eyes like my abuser. After a year of arguments and guilt, I decided to seek counseling. After three counselors, I found one who started opening closets for me. I learned that my abuse started at age six months, not to mention losing my virginity at age seven years.

As my memories continued, I became suicidal. The memories got worse, more frequent, until I couldn't cope. I wanted to end the memories so badly. The only way out; was to end my life. With the help of my support persons I got past that point. I learned what to do when a new memory arose. When I got a headache or felt tired I was watchful; then when my mind felt like it was spinning tight, I started writing my thoughts. As my embedded memory came to me, I talked it out. For a long period I never wanted to talk or write again, but I learned that was part of the healing process. There was so much inside I needed to express. Through that I found my own identity, instead of continuing to live with my abuser inside of me.

The feelings from being molested are so many, so confusing.

The intensity of each: hate, hope, betrayal, love, fear. Each feeling swarming and confused, not knowing where it fit within the producing memory, imbedding deeper after each forceful act. The forced bodily pleasure twisted among the lewd, hopeless feelings. The endless screams of silence trapped within the mind. Always looking for a new light of hope never reaching its destiny.

At age 19 I told my mother what her brutal brother did to me. The support and relief was better than I expected at first . . . Soon I felt guilty for telling. I felt as though I threw everything on their shoulders then; I felt guilty for the guilt she felt. The tension between us grew heavy. I felt as though nothing would ever go back to normal. I was mad at myself for telling. I felt as though I ruined her life. Then I learned she told family members. I felt like I was stripped of every shield I had. As a secret it had more power, I felt, for if I let the secret out I knew I could shatter and destroy every vision of a normal family.

Even with the secret out, they wouldn't let me destroy their incarnated vision. Not one word was said to me. In a way it was still a secret, except this time it was different. It left a dark cloud lingering, while my scars of pain are still hidden inside. To me they run around like a bunch of hungry ants, blinded by their own darkness. They may never know what went on for those 13 years, but the strength it took me to survive those years is more than I can say.

My family members refuse to see the truth about their beloved relative, my beloved molester. I do hold anger towards my family. I told them Uncle's "dolly" hurt me, and about the times I cried because my urine stung so bad. I had an eerie childhood, but so would they feel eerie if they could see my tangled scars.

The positive side of my incest was that it helped me help my daughter when she was molested by another sick-minded animal at age two. But that story I will leave for her to tell . . .

Today I know I can live without my family. I don't need or want anything from them, as I did when I was a child. When they want me they know where I am; if they want my story I will share it. Today I know who I am: I am a 21–year–old woman and I feel good about myself!

I feel as though I have been born again. I can enjoy my childhood years through my daughter, and the beauty of men through my husband. I am now working at a shelter for abused women and their families. I plan to go to school for training to work with sexually abused children. I want to make every effort I can to help save a child from seeing life through a victim's eyes.

My love goes out to any victim of abuse. I only know that it does get better. The tangled cobwebs can be cleaned. Self-esteem can grow so bright! My thanks goes out to every support person who stands behind a victim (especially my counselor and husband). Each of our lives can become peaceful. We can all find our own identity, and most of all, we can all be survivors!!

Beth L.

LOOKING BACK 58 YEARS

My psychiatrist had told me, repeatedly, he was certain I had been raped because of my distrust and fear of men.

One night after retiring, I thought, "If he is right, why can't I remember? I will look in the corners of my memory slowly and carefully." As I relaxed to sleep, horrible sounds came to my mind. Groans, growlings, mumblings, squeals, smacking of lips, all incoherent. I sat bolt upright. A gross fear caused my heart to pound wildly and a cold sweat to erupt on my body. I feared for my sanity.

This experience broke the seal on my memory and it all came rolling out. There seemed no way to stop it. I felt as though I were hanging by a gossamer thread to my sanity, and the slightest "bump" would tip me into lunacy. I clung to this thread for two years.

On a spring day when I was nearly five years old, I wandered to an old vacant house half a block from home. The cellar doors were open and, curious, I went in to inspect the leavings of the last tenant.

A sound of some sort, and my own apprehension made me look up toward the light in the doorway. I saw a man's legs spread wide, blocking the way. He came towards me very quickly. "Get in the corner, you brat, and keep your mouth shut." Then he hit me in the head with his fist. My heavy brown knee socks were stuffed in my mouth, obstructing my air passages and causing me to lose consciousness, which was a merciful thing, in view of the beating and raping that transpired.

My dad came home after dark, saw the light on in that cellar and came to look for me. I saw those rapist's legs go up those seven steps, only touching them once.

I had a brief moment of consciousness when they put my body in a tub of warm water and cut my dress with scissors. I saw the water was muddy blood.

This rape of their tiny daughter disgraced and frightened my parents. I was not allowed to work through my trauma, but repressed it. It haunted my dreams and affected my emotional life for 55 years. Nightmares were always the same: I could not breathe. I would wake yelling and screaming, running from a man I could not see into a cellar where there was no way out.

Because of repressing this rape-beating, I have felt powerless, afraid of everything and everyone. I was unable to develop to my potential. I will always have emotional scars from my experience. My doors are always locked at home, my car is always locked when I am in it, and when my husband is away I am apprehensive.

They never even looked for my rapist, he was never brought to justice, he is free yet. Who knows how many more victims he has had?

Anonymous

PROGRESS REPORT ON THIS AUTHOR

I saw a psychiatrist who listened to the horror I had experienced, over and over. It is very important for someone to hear you. I dumped it all on my therapist.

I have stayed away from the house and around people of my age. Walked miles in all sorts of weather — nature has such healing qualities. I have hung on. Telling myself, "I am a special person for my experience."

The worst thing has been that my husband has refused to hear any of it, wants me to forget it.

A Christmas Wish

Grandfather:

I ask a Christmas present of you
Thirty years late:

Honesty, grandfather,

honesty.

It doesn't come easily in our family.

What for us has been reality

too often has turned out to be mythology.

There's the myth about the love between us, for example:

about how cute it was that you teased me

and poked me in the stomach —

or was it my vagina?

I don't remember. I don't remember.

Something in me still wants to hold onto the myth

of the two of us sweetly going off together

to the refrigerator to share a glass of buttermilk.

Had you lived longer, grandfather,

we could have shared rum and orange juice together.

Just like I did so often with your daughter —

my mother — my abuser.

The three of us: Alcoholics.

Yes, grandfather, I inherited your addiction.

A fine Irish blessing on me now, wasn't it?

The myth that you were above that was shattered

    when the empty bottles were found in your law office

    after you died.

Grandfather:

    Tell me why my sister dreams about you

    as though you are a devil, dressed in black

    who glares at children

    and sneaks up on them when they are seeking privacy.

    Why, when she tries to remember what your home is like,

    all she sees are snakes crawling across the front lawn?

    And why throughout her life has she been attracted to

    men who walk just like you and look just like you?

Tell me about heredity, grandfather.

    And this time leave the mythology to the Greeks.

May you rest in peace, grandfather,

    but only after I rest in peace.

Sylvia

PROGRESS REPORT ON SYLVIA

I am doing quite well. I attribute that in great part to a therapist who taught me to love myself. Even when the most difficult and trying things happen in my life, there is something deep inside me that I treasure — and I survive. It took me 39 years to discover that. I have now been sober for five years and am so grateful for that.

I used to be afraid of the dark.
No one could understand why.

Erosion Of Dreams

It's dark in here, so very dark in here. Tiny three-year-old voice, terrified, alone but not alone. Intruder! With a weapon, made of flesh and gorged with blood, suspended in mid-air, poking, jabbing into the space that is my mouth. Closing off breath, forcing breath into a tight, hard center deep in my chest. Fear, a very real and substantial fear, the first thing I can consciously remember. Say it! Name the fear! Name the pain, the violation, the shame. What is your name?

(a whisper) Father.

A light. Darkness dissolves. Maybe I'll survive.

❖ ❖ ❖ ❖

Dreamed of an eagle sitting on my shoulder, nibbling at my ear like a parakeet or other pet bird. Being in a deep canyon, like the Grand Canyon, with one of my students. Explaining the making of a canyon by the force of erosion.

Barbara

PROGRESS REPORT ON BARBARA

As a teacher of the deaf, the process of healing has been difficult for me. Every time I feel healed, yet another student reports an incident of physical and/or sexual abuse to me, and it brings up new or yet-unhealed material from my own past. I also experience strong feelings of wanting to rescue the present young victim.

I have learned that, in order to survive and remain sane, progress must be seen as a series of tiny steps. I also use the idea of "planting seeds": that the small changes I am able to make now may bear fruit sometime in the future. Even though I am still on the path to healing, I feel that some things have helped me to make significant progress.

My sister, Lori, knows that I am telling the truth, and supports me. My partner, Wes, has shown me that men can be loving, gentle human beings. I remember the details of my earliest abuse incident after an intense weekend workshop with Ellen Bass. A writing workshop with Sandra Butler encouraged me to write to express my feelings, and also develop "spirit guides" to speed healing. A support group led by Deborah Cooper and Angie Romagnoli gave me the opportunity to tell my whole story — and when the world did not cave in, I felt enormously relieved and at least partly healed. Individual counseling helps. Networking with others in helping professions provides much-needed support. I find it helpful, too, to recall the words of Gibran: "The deeper sorrow carves into your being, the more joy you can contain."

Beth LaMontagne

SEVERING THE IDEALIZED FAMILY

Severing the idealized family, from the real family is like severing me into many, many pieces. Their love, however crazy and painful, is the only love there is, the only *love* I know. Now I'm supposed to survive the real world without anything. I am lonely to the core. What is going to happen when there is nothing? Is not the craziness and pain better than nothing at all?

My brain, insides, and life are crumbling at my feet, and nothing seems to be able to hold it all together. I am beginning to feel like a four-year-old orphan who is standing out in the rainy street crying "Is there nothing else, is this all there is?" I realize this is the martyr thinking, but let's face it, that is the way I feel right now. There is a four-year-old brain living in a thirty-year-old person.

I have been asking myself, "where do I go from here?" Now that all the dreams are being chipped away, bone raw reality is all that lies before me. I am unable to live in my fantasy world any longer. Feeling stripped of all escapes and so very, very, scared of the road ahead. Somehow, reality is much more frightening than the dreams I used to live with. Scared of myself and my emotions, not knowing who or what to trust, and questioning whether I can even trust myself. Help me! The smell of dead and rotting fantasies linger in my mind, making it hard to forget what has gone before; while scaring up visions of the pain to come.

Crystal Ann Jordan

A November For S.

leaves fall   like calendar pages
birds fly   leaving my sky   a blank face
deer desert the naked wood   to wander
the edges of the parkway   winter a knife
pares everything to its essential spine

i rake leaves   my doors   my windows wind-tight
i hang heavy curtains   stir
up the fire at night for you

when a thousand drunk hours fall away
eight years of calendar days   memories
begin to appear like deer on the road   stare
as you trace your footsteps back
to a child-rape   vivid white   deer in the headlights
suck in fearful air

your father's phone call set you trembling again
even the l.a. sun can't warm you   again
yesterday i saw through the woods for miles
the leaves gone   the wind   the winter's a knife
and it bites   it bites

Chela Zabin

She told her mother that she had been molested by her father.
Her mother did not do anything, even to ease the hurt.

Jana Carp

JOURNAL TO RECOVERY

I began keeping a journal when I was in therapy for severe and recurring depressions that were becoming worse with the passage of time. Eventually I was on the brink of suicide. After nearly two years of work with a gentle and intelligent therapist, I began to remember an abusive past. I was forced to give up the fantasy of a perfect childhood and come to terms with feelings of anger, betrayal, and pain for which I was not responsible, but felt as if I were.

The First Week of Remembering

I don't want to be alone today because I feel crazy. The memories I had last night are clear. How could I have forgotten? I remember waking and there was something big and looming between my legs. Moving and hurting. A hand, but whose? Don't open your eyes. Don't. Bobby. It's Bobby. Stay still. Pretend sleep. Maybe he'll go away. He hurt me with his fingernails and I felt blood between my thighs. My first blood. I don't know what it means. I was a child; not ready to bleed as a woman bleeds. Will I die? Where were you, Mommy, when Bobby touched me? I feel guilty. It is as if I did something bad, shameful. I am insane. The memories are something alien to me; something that comes from outside to hurt me. He comes back to hurt me again. I am terrified.

Week Three

Some of the fear is gone and in its place I feel dead. There is a black core deep inside me somewhere behind my heart. More than anything else I want to sit close to someone, have them put their arms around me and just be there for a while. I want someone to tell me that I wasn't a bad child, that what happened was beyond my control. I wonder why I was the one who was hurt. I would like to have some evidence that even though I was bad then, that I am not now. There is something wrong with me. If this feeling doesn't go away, I will not be able to live out my life.

Week Four

The memories of that first time with Bobby are very clear now. The room smells musty and of dogs. It was cold. The bed smelled of old urine. Why was

I sleeping at my Aunt's? When I awoke that night Bobby's hands were already on me, inside me. I was so very scared. I didn't move for a long time, kept my eyes tightly closed. My heart was pounding so hard I thought he'd hear it and know I wasn't sleeping. It's pounding now as I write this. I tried to turn over . . . pretending a little restlessness. I hoped he'd think I was going to wake up and he'd go away. He turned me gently back over. He went away after a while. I suppose he was bored or tired. He came back again later that night.

He must have known I was awake. Surely I was rigid with fear. We both pretended. There was no formal agreement, no words spoken. No "Promise me. Don't tell." Still there was an agreement and it was binding.

Week Six
I feel dirty and sick. I am afraid of being overwhelmed but sometimes think I would welcome it. I want most desperately some relief from the hurting. I am doing this to myself now. He is not here. None of them are here. I feel irrational, as if I will lose myself in another bout of useless crying, as if I will collapse upon myself. Collapsing I will find only that truncated stump of living flesh that cannot even cry out. Who will help garbage? Who would comfort shit? I feel the need to scream but have no voice. I wish I could curl myself into a tight little ball and get smaller and smaller until I disappear.

Week Eight
The questions are clear in my head. How did I make it happen? I must have deserved it. But why? I am unable to make much sense of what has been happening to me. I must be going crazy.

Week Ten
I have been thinking of that person to whom awful things happened as someone else. And I don't like her. She is nasty and soiled. She is less than a person; not quite human. Humans are loved. I hate the part of myself that feels sorry for her. She had too many things wrong with her. A part of me wants to kill her.

I think with the rational part of myself that I want to change that suicidal feeling. I want to put that feeling away with a lot of other feelings that have no place in my life. The rational part of myself struggles for control. Will I ever be whole?

Week Eleven

When I remembered nothing it was a problem; not remembering made life impossible. Remembering is impossible too. Isn't it as difficult to see when there is too much light as it is when there is darkness?

Sometimes I can venture a little way out and just let happen what will happen. When I open myself that way, when I can just be, each moment can be a little gift to myself. I dare not look for those gifts; they come unexpectedly like a flock of cedar wax wings that are there and gone in a moment of beautiful confusion. If I spend my life waiting for cedar wax wings I am doomed to disappointment. The kind of moments I mean are small and warm and happen only when I am able to shut down the defenses and be an accepting observer.

Last New Year's Day we went to the beach. It was cold and windy and clear. The wind blew straight into the surf. The waves were huge and as they curled into the beach the wind caught them and blew a fine spray back and up. When the combination was just right, when light, wind and surf came together, a rainbow formed off the top of a wave. It was always happening just at the corner of my vision. I could not see it by watching for it. I just had to take my chances. It was a wonderful, beautiful day.

I cannot force that to happen. I can only try to be aware that the moments are happening and watch for them out of the corners of my awareness.

Week Twelve

I wonder how disclosing my memories will affect my family, my friends. Will they respond as I do with revulsion and disgust? And really, what I have remembered so far is a very mild cruelty compared to what some others have. I don't know what to do with even this little abuse that seems so big. I don't think I have all the pieces yet.

A small abuse. A small child. I always thought that I was not pretty. Even ugly. Today I look at pictures of that thin, freckled eight-year-old whose auburn braids stretched halfway down her back. She seems pretty and her hazel eyes look into the camera from an intelligent face. What does that mean?

Last night I remembered again with an eight-year-old's mind in that time before sleep when one is never sure whether it is sleep or wakefulness. I felt again with terror, with hurt, with bewilderment, as the shameful, painful touching began again. The happening was now, not then. The pain was real; it was immediate. Bobby was touching the most secret part of my eight-year-old body.

The place so hidden, so private that it had no name. The place was not real because it was nameless. He was hurting me and couldn't be because my body had no such place to hurt.

"Mommy, what is he doing?" I called myself awake.

Every once in a while today the memory would come and mix in confusing ways with self-abnegation, a sense that it was not true, not real. Perhaps I made it up. But I didn't. I know that my sisters and cousins were molested too. Every one of us children knew. Eight kids were hurt and never cried, never told. Even among ourselves we kept the secret. I kept it till it was gone. Forgotten. My body remembered what my mind forgot. My body kept the secret and gave back stomach aches and eating problems. Black depressions and incapacitating dependencies. Deep inside I knew I was not good, know it now, and have as evidence early experiences laid down as firmly, as immutably as a geological layer of silt pressed by time and pressure until finally it becomes stone.

Week Fourteen

More remembering last night. This time it was Uncle Pug touching my breasts. I was about 12 and didn't even have real breasts. Mine were more like buds then, brand new and tender to touch. I remembered Uncle Dick too — the time he tried to get me in his bed "for just a little good-night kiss." I remember him kissing me with his mouth open and his hands holding my body against him. I was ten.

Until today I thought I liked Uncle Al. He is tall and slender and so handsome. He has bright blue eyes. Happy eyes that are intelligent. He is funny, kind and gentle. Every time I saw him, every time any of my sisters saw him, he touched us. If you were standing he hugged you and ran his hands over your buttocks. If you were sitting he put his hand on your knee and rubbed it and ran his hand over your leg.

"That was for luck," he'd say, and his hands and face would smile. He'd wink at my dad and say, "That's good stuff. Chicken." They'd exchange nods or "good ol' boy" nudges in the ribs. Mom would smile. Everyone liked Uncle Al. He belonged to the bishop's honor guard. He had one of those silly plumed hats and a sword. I thought I liked Uncle Al until today when thinking about it made me very angry. Today I wished he'd fall on his sword and hurt and hurt and hurt the way I do.

I mastered the form of life. I was very, very good. I was polite. I obeyed the rules. I hoped for meaning. I waited for the hurt to stop. I learned to trust no one because inside the child-me knew the truth. I knew I was bad. It felt crazy. Feels crazy. I know I am worthless. I am not innocent. I've always known. The good are not hurt the way I was hurt.

Week Fifteen

I am sorry. Not the sympathetic sorry. The apologetic sorry. I am sorry that I am not stronger, better, purer, cleaner, prouder, smarter. I am sorry I never told anyone my dirty little secret. I'm sorry I remembered it.

Week Sixteen

Today I asked my friend for forgiveness. Forgive me for being evil. Forgive me for not being innocent. Forgive me for all of it. Please. She said, "I will not forgive you. Not ever. Never." Blackness began to swarm around me, despair to choke me. I felt her hand on my face, lifting my chin to look in her eyes; her arms around me, a safe envelope. "There is nothing to forgive," she said. "You never did anything wrong."

The first step in my healing was taken then. I was absolutely astonished. It wasn't my fault! I had done nothing.

I am not a religious person but I am deeply and profoundly spiritual. What I felt that night with my friend, my teacher, was Goodness. It was as if I were carrying a hard dry sponge around inside me that suddenly began to fill with warmth and to spread. Over the next few days I became aware that I was quiet inside. The static, the rumbling, with which I had always distracted myself was fading. I was filled with calm, with peace and a deep sense of my potential strength. It was pure, childlike in its openness and in its innocence. I felt benevolence, grace, human-to-human love both personal and universal. Holy. I am humbled by the strength of that outpouring. I am awed, full of wonder. I think I have made some of that goodness permanent inside me.

It is a slow, difficult struggle, one that goes on for me. Sometimes the blackness does begin to come back as more and more comes out of my memory, but I am stronger now. I have stared into the face of Evil and Evil looked away first.

April 1985

During the time following the writings above I have had the opportunity to speak with many people about sexual abuse and its effects on the survivor. I have often felt myself to be in the role of Paul Revere galloping about the countryside calling, "The British are coming. The British are coming." But instead of the Minutemen hurrying to the defense of their homes, they stand in their doorways and lean from their windows and say, "Shut up. I hate war. Don't tell me about it." But I have been wounded in this war. I have nearly died of my hurts. The scars will never go away. They are part of who I am.

What then do I want? I do not want to waste my pain. I want it to count. I want justice. Not revenge. Punishment is not justice. I want the abusers, the inflicters of pain to experience their consciences, to look inside themselves and feel what I feel. That would be justice. And I want anger. I want a public outcry. I want someone to be angry for me. To be angry for their sons and daughters. To be angry enough to endure the painful listening. Be angry enough to make it stop.

Suzanne

PROGRESS REPORT ON SUZANNE

I continue to work on my abuse issues, and my memory still gives me pieces to fit into the puzzle of my childhood. My healing is happening in the midst of loving support. Most helpful to me have been contacts with other childhood abuse victims. The powerful support of these women gives me the courage to do the work I need to do.

Recovery has taken the form of helping other women and men heal from the wounds of violence. I have been active in the battered women's movement — first as a volunteer, then full time as a women's advocate and presently as a member of the Board of Directors of New Hope for Women in Maine.

I am now employed as a substance abuse counselor, where my clients are often adult survivors of childhood sexual and physical abuse.

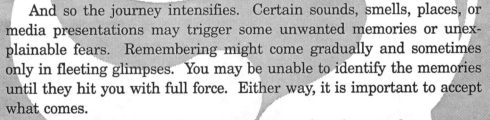

INSIGHTS AND PERCEPTIONS

And so the journey intensifies. Certain sounds, smells, places, or media presentations may trigger some unwanted memories or unexplainable fears. Remembering might come gradually and sometimes only in fleeting glimpses. You may be unable to identify the memories until they hit you with full force. Either way, it is important to accept what comes.

Sometimes the remembering seems as real as the actual experience. Although the feelings are presently intense, realize that you are now in control. Remember, that was then and this is now. It would also be very beneficial to seek out the help you couldn't ask for or receive then.

Reliving these memories, however they come, is emotionally draining. So take extra care of yourself emotionally as well as physically. Take naps, soak in the tub, listen to peaceful music, find some healthy physical activity to help diffuse this powerful energy. Allow yourself the right to be whoever you need to be.

BE NURTURING

CHAPTER EIGHT

STARTING OVER

"I would not, under any circumstances, trade the pain of today for the pain of yesterday. The pain of healing, while not easy to cope with, is more bearable than the pain of hurt."

Marsha Allen

THE FENCE

The grass may not be greener on the other side of the fence. I know what it is on this side, the pain and sorrow. The scars are so deep, I don't even feel the pain, the joy, or laughter. If I cross the fence, the people on the other side may find another spot without scars, and then I will feel a new and different pain.

The scars and pain make me so heavy, I have no strength to climb the fence. Sometimes I can't even see the fence for the tears clouding my eyes. The pain here is bearable. I know what to expect. Over there, what would it be like? How would I survive?

I have never known freedom. I might only find another slaver to take care of me and abuse me again. Is there any relief from bondage? Do I need to cross that fence? Where can I find the strength to cross?

Lou Battams

LAURA'S STORY

I never thought of the relationship with Doc as being abusive, even when as an adult I became knowledgeable about sexual abuse. Chronologically I was an adult. He cared about me and said he would never hurt me. In the end when I said "no more," the physical side of our relationship ended. Doc taught me a lot about life and my feelings. It was a very special relationship, but one I knew not to talk about and didn't for a long time.

A year ago I told our marriage counselor about the relationship with Doc. It had been a long time since I had even thought about the physical involvement we had once had. It has been difficult to look at Doc, my professor, advisor and friend, as a sex offender, and myself as one of his victims. For a long time it was easier to believe it was at least partially my responsibility.

I was just 18 and incredibly naive when I left home to attend a private Christian college. In biology I had learned all the body parts well and in church the "Thou shall nots," but there was a large gap when it came to information about feelings. I was left very vulnerable, though I never knew that until recently.

I met Doc the first week of school when I needed to see him about transferring into his class. He had a delightful sense of humor and was always willing to help. There were no "dumb" questions to him, whether it related directly to class or not. I enjoyed his class and his openness, so I requested him as my academic advisor at the end of the semester.

At the beginning of my second year, I attended a retreat where I was abruptly confronted with my own sexual naiveté. I went to the one person I really trusted, Doc, for information. There was so much that I didn't know, and he was very willing to share what he knew. I also had long talks with his wife as I got to know his family. It was quite a year as my own awareness grew and with it a new self-confidence. Doc made me feel so special and accepted. If I had been more aware, I might have thought I was in love with him.

When I came back my Junior year, I got a new work-study job as a teacher's assistant working for Doc. I enjoyed working for him, and it also gave me reason to see him frequently. I still had a lot of questions about this sexual being awakening within me. The touching started casually but didn't stay that way.

He said he wanted me to know the feelings a woman had. So he massaged my breasts, at first with my clothes on and eventually with undoing my bra and blouse. It felt good, whatever it was that went on inside me. I believed him when he told me how special I was and how great it was to see me so responsive. I had doubts about the touching and fondling; something must be wrong if we needed to hide. He reassured me that everything was okay; some people might not understand, but who was it hurting? I had no evidence it was hurting anyone, and I had to agree it felt good. We used his office, his car, and occasionally his family room for our meetings. As we got more involved physically, we talked less — and that concerned me. I didn't want the good things I experienced to get in the way of the wonderful discussions we used to have.

I remember it started one night when I called his home to let everyone know I was back from vacation. Doc wanted to see me, tonight, to discuss a letter I had sent him over vacation. Would I meet him so we could go to his office? I couldn't believe my own words when I said yes. I had written him to say I wanted to cut back on the touching and now I was agreeing to meet him at night, alone, in the building.

As I stood waiting for him, my mind went over the routine. First a big hello hug and an invitation to come in. As I'd step inside his office, he'd pull the door shut behind me and turn the lock. There were usually some light comments passed back and forth as he'd get comfortable in his chair. He'd signal me to come sit, and when I did, he'd carefully unclip my bra. Gently he would slide his hand under my top, find my breast and start to rub it. As I relaxed and let the warm feelings flow, I'd lean my head on his shoulder. Recently he had been taking my hand and placing it on his crotch so I could feel his hard, erect penis. I didn't like it, but he reminded me of how much he did for me — couldn't I do this one thing for him? I couldn't say no.

Now he walked up, and there was the familiar greeting. The quiet darkness enclosed us as we entered the building to go up to his office. He turned on the small desk lamp in the office, and then spread a coat on the floor. Something felt different as he asked me to sit beside him on the floor. We talked for a while about my letter. He explained that one can't back up a relationship; one can only go forward. Once again he assured me that what we did didn't hurt anyone. I objected as he undid my bra and he reassured me again. I lost my resistance as my body began to respond to his touch. He eased me on to my back, and then laid on top of me. I didn't understand his rocking back and forth. My face must have shown it for he told me just to lie still. I did as I was told. He got off a few minutes later, leaving a wet spot on my pants and his.

I knew then what had happened but not why. I wanted out. I was scared. He wanted to talk and make sure I was okay. I lied when he asked. I just wanted to go wash. Footsteps in the hall stalled any hope of leaving quickly. What would happen to me, to Doc, if someone found us now; our usual alibi of working wouldn't hold up very well this time.

There was a new conviction after that night that much as I enjoyed it, the touching needed to stop. I wasn't ready to give up the friendship, especially with his family, but I did need some distance from Doc. I made arrangements to quit my T.A. position, explaining to anyone who needed to know that I needed the time more than the money. There was enough truth in it so as to not arouse any suspicions. I missed the attention, but a growing sense of guilt over what happened kept me from going by his office.

Several months later I met Doc on campus, and he asked me to ride along to pick up some things at his boat. As we rode, the conversation was general at first, but then changed to how much he had missed me. I began to get uneasy as he went on talking about how special I was to him. I walked the deserted dock to the boat with a knot in my stomach.

In spite of my objections, he undressed me in the forward cabin. He left me just my panties and a light blanket while he went to undress. He returned, pausing briefly in the doorway. He was stark naked. His penis was large and erect. I had never seen a man's penis, and I couldn't quite believe how large it was. Even his warm smile could not slow my racing heart now. How stupid I had been to come. There was little doubt that he wanted more than to just fondle my breasts. He tried to be gentle, but I didn't even want to be touched. I don't know how long we were there — it seemed like forever. He eventually left and threw me my clothes. It was easy enough to tell he was angry. I didn't want to hurt him, but I really believed intercourse before marriage was wrong. I was scared that "it" might just happen. He said everything was okay but I could tell he was upset.

The fondling stopped after that. I wanted to forget all of it. I took my diary and a black marker and lined out the references to Doc. I hoped it was a way to forgive and forget and move on.

The friendship with Doc and his family has continued to the present, and now also includes my husband and children. I have struggled in the past year to come to grips with being a victim of sexual abuse. My husband knows the story and my offender and he provide good support. We are working together to rebuild a happy, healthy sex life. The sex education of my children has taken on a new sense of urgency. As I regain my power, I am trying to use it in positive ways to help others.

I still live with the paradoxes, trying to find a balance point. To accept that Doc is and was a good friend, advisor, teacher, and *a sex offender* is hard. To believe he really did care about me and really did sexually abuse me is a strange contradiction. I live in celebration that he did dispell my naiveté and mourn that he victimized me.

Laura

PROGRESS REPORT ON LAURA

The reality of being a victim of sexual abuse doesn't come all at once. Neither does seeing the many ways it taints the present. I am learning to live a day at a time. I have returned to therapy to work on issues within my marriage, my sexuality, and unresolved questions about the sexual abuse. Often they ended up being the same. It has taken both time and work to find freedom.

I found healing in sharing my story with family and friends. In talking about the abuse I hear a reality that the silence of the secret does not reveal. It was my mother's anger and grief that gave me a new permission to be angry at what had happened.

When I found out I was not Doc's only victim, I needed to know it was not still happening to others. The confrontation was very difficult. He told his wife of my "accusations." Both were outraged and minimized what had happened. He did say that he knew that "technically" our relationship had been abusive, but he had always loved me and never wanted to hurt me. It was the end of the friendship. I grieve the loss, and that the confrontation needed to happen. It is another paradox to live with.

The other paradoxes still exist (maybe they always will). The balance is there most days. The road of recovery takes both work and time, and it happens a day at a time.

LETTER UNMAILED

My Dear Friend,

You asked, "Why would anyone want to be touched?"
Your question haunts me
and knowing (recognizing) the underlying question
"How can you forget 'the touch'?"
prompts an answer.

I am blessed that only the "Statue Girl" was touched.
She is the only one that truly remembers
the incidents of my childhood —
and I put her to sleep years ago.
Occasionally she awakes
and to put her at ease
I list my "thank you's" to God.
I touch my husband;
stroke his warm fuzzy body
and thank God for his presence in my life.
I was alone
isolated,
afraid to venture from my self-sealed walls
and he has listened gently
and (as much as a male can),
has understood.
He remembers and tries to picture
the terror of a young girl
afraid to go to the bathroom
for fear of being cornered and fondled.
I touch him as we make love,
consciously thanking God for his love,
for his ability to assume responsibility
for my fatherless children.

I thank God for blessing me with a man
who is willing to do housework
so I can pursue any one of my compulsive hobbies.
I stroke his arms
and thank God that the arms *were there*
to hold and comfort me.
I brush his cheek
and thank God that he always turns it
when I am offensive to him.

I rub his shoulders,
loving the closeness that I feel
and thank God that I am able to enjoy that;
Finally, my friend . . .
I pray. "Dear Lord, help me forget the past right now and focus all my
energies on this man who has done so much to help me grow. Help me enjoy
the other kind of touch."

Sandra A. Bjorkman

PROGRESS REPORT ON SANDRA

The once "impending cloud of doom" that seemed to hang over my life
is gone now. I have worked hard to make it go away. I've involved myself,
and my family (including my very supportive husband Keith) in many different
therapy processes. I've seen my therapists and have been in several group
therapy processes. Keith also went to a group for several months that was for
husbands of abuse victims. He gained much understanding and could see how
"we" relate to many of life's experiences in similar ways.

My journey/struggle is not over — it may never be over. Nearly every day
I face a past paranoia that I need to work out. I fight insecurity, and fear of
success and the spotlight success brings. But I can look at my list of things that
I have overcome and I am encouraged.

Today I teach first grade and daily share a personal safety curriculum with
my students. I am pleased that I can tell children to say *no*. I am currently
working on my own book, *He Touched Me,* which is a Christian testimony of how
God's plan has worked for me and how He can work for others.

TO THE LITTLE GIRL
I NEED TO FIND AGAIN

Your eyes are glistening, stinging from your crying
And your little arms are reaching out for me
I cannot move from hell until I find you
I cannot mend my heart till you're at peace

I am the only one who cares and can free you
I am your only key to put your shame behind
If my arms were only long enough to reach you
Then maybe peace and love is what we'd find

I want to die when I envision your tormenting
I want to kill the bastards who used your innocence
I want to hide you in my arms and calm your sobbing
But right now I cut myself and bleed instead

I will keep on searching till I have you with me
And I pray to God that soon we both will see
That the pain doesn't have to take us over
And little child, maybe then we'll be set free

Rylee Brown

It seems like I've spent my lifetime looking for a caring, gentle adult who'd listen to me and offer me comfort from my tears and fears. I just wanted to be held and know someone cared.

Anonymous

FADED MEMORIES

How do I begin to describe the memories that are so faded now, yet somewhere etched deep in my soul I know are a reality? All the wasted and troubled years — if only I could turn back the clock, but then I wouldn't be the person I am today, with such growth to measure.

Where does it begin? Is it one's destiny, or is one just a victim of circumstance? Did it begin with a very abusive husband, or as a lonely child searching to be loved? One might say that it was being approached in a sexual manner when I was twelve, and that although I wasn't physically hurt, the fear and confusion left emotional scars. For me, I think they are all entwined.

I have faded memories of a childhood that by all outward appearances should have been good, but I was always overwhelmed by a haunting emptiness. I was the oldest of seven children. My father worked long and hard; my mother was always home tending to the house and little ones. Each one of us seemed somewhat detached and aloof.

My encounter at twelve left me stunned and bewildered. That one rare afternoon when my Dad and I were home alone, he explained to me about men's physical urges. He drew me close, but although he didn't "touch" me, I was an object for his self-gratification. "Oh God, why is he putting me through this?" I was so confused, I started to faint.

I never told anyone, I suppose out of a sense of loyalty and love. I didn't want to cause anyone any pain, or have someone think badly of him and me. Besides, putting it into words might have made it more of a reality. The fear of that one incident slowly faded and we actually, in time, became fairly close, which seemed contradictory. Maybe secrets bind people together, but how can a true and good relationship develop if not built on trust and honesty?

One day in our family pool, my sister screamed, her hands reaching towards me, as our father drew her close. "Oh no, not her!" Oh why did I turn away? I later heard whispers of it happening to my other sister as well. Oh, the guilt I carried, and how well I blocked it all from my thoughts. Though I wasn't physically hurt, the wheels were set in motion.

I have faded memories of two innocent 16-year-olds, both searching to fill an empty void. I think we both knew what would happen that night but I felt awful,

I didn't want to go through with it. "I'm so afraid, I don't want to do this, no, don't." Why couldn't I have been more forceful?

Through that one union came a pregnancy, a marriage, a daughter. First there were the jealousies, shoves, then the slaps, and by the time my daughter was two the beatings never stopped. "Oh, she was so good. She knew when to retreat to her own room for her own safety, and withdraw to a world of fantasy."

My seven-year marriage was a bizarre hell. I can't begin to describe the insanities. I was brainwashed, a puppet, a possession. I was forced to submit to sex at least every day, sometimes twice. It didn't matter that some days I was so physically bruised and in pain; to withhold meant a guaranteed beating.

After my son was born, something changed in me. I couldn't let him grow up seeing his mother being abused and possibly becoming an abuser. I thank God for the strength to walk away. As my children became ten and eleven, I felt myself pulling away, and avoiding any physical contact. Oh, how could I have been so afraid to give my children a loving hug? Had I never been shown when I was young?

The next ten years were filled with loneliness, illicit affairs, suicidal depressions, tranquilizers, anti-depressants, unexplained emotional outbursts and tears. Oh, why couldn't I have been able to say no to a man? Why couldn't I have been more in control of my own body, and not let myself get into situations I could not let myself get out of? Or so I thought! I only attached myself to the ones who were unavailable, immature, or had as many emotional problems as myself. I got a job bartending, which only put more emphasis on sexuality, and added the feeling of prostituting. I knew if I smiled a little more or talked a little longer, business and tips would increase. By the time I was 25 I had cervical cancer, and a hysterectomy, which only added to a feeling of inadequacy.

Somehow I began to realize that the sexual encounters left me feeling even emptier, and I went through a period of pulling away from men. I learned to be alone without being lonely, to like and love myself. I'm still working on the guilt of putting my work first, my emotional attachment second, and my two wonderful children third!

I've been married five years now to the most wonderful man. My story should end here, but it's only the beginning. The beginning of balancing energies. Getting married stirred up many subconscious feelings. My hidden resentments towards men surfaced and were directed towards my husband. I was afraid of being manipulated and controlled. Therapy helped me to realize that I was worthy of a good and lasting relationship.

As things got better, and my husband and I became closer, my daughter, now married and having problems, came to me with the shocking secret that my own brother had sexually molested her for six years when she was young. No words can describe my pain. My own personal experience became all the more vivid in my mind and for the first time I told someone, my daughter. I had a hard time separating my daughter and friend from my little girl that had been hurt. I confronted my brother on four occasions and begged him to go for help.

My feelings went through stages. The very first feeling was wanting to protect my brother and hating my daughter for telling me this. "Oh why did she let it happen?" After the shock came denial; then I just tried to ignore it, hoping all would be as it was. Therapy with a wonderful woman helped me to realize that everything wouldn't be the same, but I could make it better.

After six months of being eaten up alive, I almost destroyed my marriage again. I hated sex and its animal urges. I finally told my husband about my daughter. He was so understanding and supportive, I wish I had told him sooner. Next, I talked with my sisters about everything. I even shared my guilt feelings for turning away that day. I then talked to my parents, now divorced. It's hard for my Mom to face the realities of life she chose to ignore.

My Dad actually made it easy. We talked about the past and my sisters, how the incidents are still affecting us, his emotional turmoil, and my brother. We both had a good cry, and laid the foundation for a new and honest relationship.

As we all were building our lives again, my beautiful two-and-a-half-year-old granddaughter was molested by an acquaintance. My daughter recognized the symptoms, really listened to what others might perceive as idle chatter, and got professional help. I felt so ripped apart, this reaching to three generations. We are fairly sure she will be fine, mainly because it wasn't kept a secret. This latest experience also helped me to understand that it wasn't my fault for not knowing what was happening to my daughter years before.

I'm almost through with my therapy. I've come so far, released so many secrets, and I'm finding that the more doors I unlock, the more expressive and creative I become, and more "alive." I still have my rough days, dealing with guilt for not being there more for my children, and for pushing them away at a time when they needed so much love and support. In the dark of night I still battle the inner turmoil as I try to separate thoughts and memories of others' secret desires and self-gratification from my husband's loving touch.

But where does it begin? An unspoken word, a feeling, an example, an outside influence? I'm told this can be hereditary, and it surely touched the lives of three generations that I know of, but hopefully with the release of secrets we have brought this to an end. In writing this I have been reminded of the destructiveness of secrets, and realize that I have one more secret to disclose. I must collect enough faith, trust and strength to share my childhood experience with my husband. He has proved his loyalty, patience, and understanding, yet I have held back in fear, while knowing deep in my soul that sharing the real me, being truly vulnerable to his love, could only bring contentment.

My daughter, my sister and myself are living proof that good can come from misfortunes if you truly believe in yourself, and dare to be all of who you are.

These memories aren't so faded now as I retrace the steps of my soul, but in time these may forever become . . . only faded memories.

Just Another Survivor

PROGRESS REPORT ON THIS AUTHOR

I completed a year of therapy about eleven months ago. In the beginning I remember feeling depressed and thinking that there was something wrong with me. I'd have to tell myself, "No, I'm seeking help and getting stronger." I remember the first couple of visits asking, "What am I doing here?" Then I began to think of my therapist as a good friend. I looked forward to seeing her, for I always felt better afterwards. She helped me to deal with my daughter's abuse, and then my granddaughter's.

I am glad I talked to my Dad about my own experience. Our relationship is pretty good, but I can see how two of my sisters carry strong resentment and bitterness to this day; they have never really tried to deal with their situations. I have not confronted my brother anymore, not because I'm trying to avoid it, but because I just don't have a need to at this time.

I started asking questions and investigating, and found four generations of sexual abuse in my family — of my granddaughter, daughter, myself, sisters, Mom and aunts. Abusers are on my Mom's side of the family as well.

One thing my therapist did, which I felt helped, was when I got upset or couldn't deal with a particular issue, she would have me talk about it over and over until it was more a "matter of fact," and didn't carry such emotional charge. She also helped me realize it took a lot of energy to keep my secrets hidden.

I did tell my husband about my secrets, and had him read my story. He was very compassionate. There are times when I still feel sexual distance, but he understands and doesn't take it personally.

There may come a time, whether it is a month or a year from now, when I may need and be ready for additional help. But for now I feel healed, with added strength, depth, and energy to tackle life's everyday lessons and challenges.

VICTIM/OFFENDER

I have been a victim of sexual abuse, mental and emotional. I have also been the offender. I was with my mother for the first three years of my life. I know very little of those years except that she drank a lot and would end up leaving me in various places. These places were abandoned cars and alleys. The police would end up with me and she would take me back. Less is known of my father. I never met him.

During these first three years there was a great deal of emotional and physical abuse, the worst being that I did not learn the basics of love, caring, trust, giving and receiving. I also never learned the basic skills of being social. I experienced emotional pain, rejection, hurt and fear from those around me. I felt this to such a degree that I turned off my feelings and detached myself from them. Much had to be pushed inside.

Because of the abuse I was experiencing, my aunt and her husband adopted me at age three. These people raised me from this point until I was eleven years old, when my aunt died. I am sure now that if it was not for her care and love I would have become a much more destructive and dangerous sex offender.

During the years with this couple I showed many signs of needing serious professional help. I would laugh at times when my aunt would cry. Her sad feelings would reach me but would be twisted and not channeled in a healthy way. I would push people away, yet would not want them to go. I believe I began acting out my sex-offender feelings at around five or six years of age. My adopted sister, who was much older than myself, would let me sleep with her from time to time. At one time, I tried to crawl up her nightgown — not being curious but in releasing some twisted feeling. She awoke and I got in trouble. I got some special attention.

Around age eight or nine, my acting out of feelings was directed towards younger children. As I remember, this brought more special attention. I felt guilty and bad. At this same age, I, myself, was sexually abused by a much older male. Again I felt guilty for some reason, but I also felt good about the physical contact. It felt nice to be touched. From 8 to 14 years, I was abused by two more males. I lived in a world of guilt, feeling I was the only bad person around.

By the time I turned 12, I had sexually abused three younger female children of families I was with. I also abused one younger male. When I was 13 my step mother, in an alcoholic condition, tried to seduce me.

My period of being emotionally and sexually abused as a child and adolescent was over. It was not until the age of 23 or 24 that I started sexually offending again, and this time the focus was on female adolescents and adults. This acting out started one year after I was married. I also started drinking alcohol again. I did not have any idea of my feelings inside or what was going on with me. I had no concept of my being a valuable person or that other people were valuable. I started acting out by picking up hitchhikers and ordering them to remove their clothes. I did this for a long time, then started exposing myself and other such forms of abuse. All this offending went on for a year and a half. Then I was arrested for sexual abuse.

I was able to get into the only sex offender program in my state. Having the behavioral and emotional problems that make up most sex offenders, I also had the denial problems. I told myself and others that I would not offend again. I really believed this and meant it. Unfortunately, it was based on nothing. I had not made any changes, nor increased my knowledge of myself. Like any other serious problem, I didn't want to accept the part of me that hurt other people and myself.

I eventually was released and was back with my wife. Within a few months I was acting out again. I was returned to the hospital; I knew the games to play and was soon released. Within the year I was arrested again.

I was sent back to the hospital. At this point I had no idea what to do. Faking and lying my way through did not work, plus I did not want to hurt anyone else again. This time I did not move through the program for a number of years. During these years, with the help of many people on the hospital staff, I slowly started making some very basic changes. Changes such as getting in touch with my feelings, accepting myself and being honest about what I'd done, handling feelings appropriately, and slowly learning to trust other people. This was very, very hard. It has all been hard.

Eventually I was released again. I have been out now for five years and have not harmed another person. I still have the ability to hurt others, but the changes I've made so far have kept my behavior constructive. I do many forms of volunteer work directed towards helping others help themselves. It is in no way easy but it is much better than what my life was before.

Merle

MARSHA'S STORY

My first memory of life outside the womb is of lying in a stark white bassinet and realizing I had some control over my right arm. The next memory is of being picked up out of the bassinet with a jerk and having a strange tasting, warm object forced into my mouth. I felt like I could not breathe and no matter how hard I tried I could not make my right arm work for me this time.

Finally, by jerking my head back and forth, the object popped out of my mouth. I started to cry. My mother screamed, "What are you doing to her?" Thud! I landed back in the bassinet and heard my uncle answer, "You never mind what I'm doing . . . and I'll do anything I want to." Next I heard a slap and my mother landing on a floor. Then an eerie silence . . . I had stopped crying without noticing. A zipper was zipped, heavy steps headed across the room. The door was opened and slammed shut. My uncle had gone and my mother was still on the floor, only now she was crying.

It seems like I lay there for a long time, listening, before she picked me up with absent-minded arms and held me, with little feeling, next to her. She held me too close under her breast. My face was pushed against her rough wool sweater and I had trouble breathing. It was December, 1945. My uncle had brought over our Christmas presents.

My sudden introduction to the adult world came when I was about three months old. The molesting and raping would go on for the next 21 years and would involve in some way the entire family on my mother's side. The perpetrators' moral code restrained them from raping me until after I had "given myself" to my high school boyfriend. I was 16. My uncle, husband of my mother's older sister, molested my brother also and taught him how to molest me. My brother is two and one-half years older than I am and was always stronger and bigger. He used me as his prime target for releasing his frustration and anger. Dad was a drunk for the first six years of my life. When he gave that up, he chased women, when away from home, and withdrew into himself at home. He was aware of my brother molesting me from the time I was two. Mom's advice to me when I was seven was that this was something that I would have to put up with and when I grew up I would get married and be very happy. I bought both myths.

One method of coping during these years was to try and please the hell out of anyone and everyone. Other methods included food and a very strong denial system. In both grade school and high school I had many friends and won social honors, but never academic ones. There was seldom any mental room left in my mind to figure out algebra problems or to explain the meaning of "All roads lead to Rome." My mind needed to work on keeping the secret buried, both from the public and from myself.

After learning that there was only enough money to send one of us to college (which of course was my brother), I willingly gave up trying to be studious and started learning typing and shorthand. A job would give me the freedom to move away from the abusive atmosphere in which I lived. Perhaps this was the first true step in my recovery. Perhaps my parents had that in mind.

At age 18 and with the security of a good job, I wanted the raping and humiliation to stop. In order to make this happen I had to hold a loaded shotgun to my brother's head and three years later pulled a hunting knife on my uncle. I was heard. It was now time to get on with my life and forget the past.

Once on my own, I lost myself in being drunk and smoking dope. At age 26 I gave up drinking; I still smoke dope. This worked on the surface but I knew I was unhappy. While in my mid-twenties I went to see a psychologist, a man. The incest and abuse never came up. Looking back I see that at that time I did not feel safe enough to face it. Also, I met my husband-to-be and knew once we were married I would be happy.

But we weren't happy. After seven and a half years of being miserable together, my husband and I entered marriage counseling. My temper was way out of control and so was my husband's drinking. The incest was not an issue at this time because I did not remember it. This time the counselor was a woman, a registered clinical social worker with a master's degree. We, I in particular, struck gold. It took a couple of years until we, my husband and I, felt like we were involved with each other in a positive manner rather than negative.

Right after high school I went to work for Pacific Northwest Bell and then for Pacific Power & Light. Fourteen years in all, I did the office routine and rarely used the typing skills I had tried so hard to learn. The shorthand skills were never called upon and are now completely forgotten. In 1977 I quit the corporate world, stayed home for a year, then went to work as a part-time employee for the company owned by the abusing uncle and his immediate family.

Pressure was put on me by my aunt about my strained relationship with my mother. As a result of this pressure I severed all ties with my mother in 1979 and in the spring of 1980 quit my job. Several attempts were made on the part of my aunt and her daughter to "make me" see my mother, but my continual refusal wore them down. My mother calls about once a year. Some years it is my husband she calls, some years it is me (usually around my birthday). Her frequent comment is, "Why do you hate me?" My reaction is always to hang up. Should her words ever change, I might listen.

In the fall of 1981, my brother contacted me from Los Angeles to tell me he was in the hospital for psychiatric care. He clearly wanted my support for his endeavors. For a while I begrudgingly gave it and hated myself, for what I wasn't quite sure. The years of abuse were never mentioned. With the realization that I didn't want to and had no obligation to help and support him came personal strength. In a letter to my brother I related the only incident of being molested by him or my uncle I could recall. I was around eight or nine at the time and my brother and I were alone in a trailer house that belonged to my Dad's cousin. Compared to what I have remembered since this particular time, that incident was very mild. Why I recalled this single instance from so many years of abuse at that particular time may never be clear to me. But I did remember and strongly felt the humiliation of it. In the letter, I also told my brother I had to sort this incident between us out, and that I would contact him, he was not to contact me. So far he has honored my request.

Without my family around to remind me with their presence that there was a secret to be kept, it was easier for me to acknowledge that there was a secret. Now I could look at my mother and her family with an emotional as well as a physical distance. I am freer, but still tied.

At this present stage of my recovery I hold no plans to ever see my family again. My dad died when I was 21; the remainder of the abusers are alive. I feel they don't deserve to be around me. My anger and hatred is so great that I don't feel it would be good for my health to see them. There would only be more denial and I don't want to hear from them ever again.

The memories of a childhood filled with sexual abuse and emotional turmoil, memories not once recalled in 15 years, started to return in April, 1982. The freedom from work outside my home, the distance I had put between my family and myself, my improved marriage and joining a women's support group led to my living a more secure and peaceful lifestyle, thus triggering the flood of memories which are still coming out today, almost four years later.

Another trigger that helped open the door on my memories was my reading about Vietnam. I did not just read a book or two, but over thirty, and one right after the other. My husband is a Vietnam veteran. In order to understand what had happened to him, I needed to learn about the war. But the more I read the more I was starting to "feel" Vietnam and even had war dreams. Because trauma victims share many of the basic feelings, no matter what caused them, I began to identify my own trauma feelings through reading about the lives of Vietnam vets. The writers of those books will never know they helped an incest victim get in touch with her feelings. I am sure if it were not for those books my recovery would have taken much longer.

The women's support group I attend once a week is headed by the same woman who counseled my husband and me. Belonging to this group helps me to recall the memories of abuse. One night at the group I talked about being afraid of the dark when I was seven years old, but I could not remember what made me afraid of it. At home that night, when I tried to tell my husband about being afraid of the dark, I started to cry. Suddenly this changed to being very afraid someone was coming to get me, and I didn't know who. I was experiencing my first flashback. All the terror and anguish of being molested by my uncle, one particular night 29 years earlier, came back to me that evening.

At this point in my life, the women in the support group are the main women in my life. I have found that friends in the real world don't necessarily stay through thick and thin. The group has provided me with a safe and trusting environment in which I can unload some of the burden being an incest victim brings. I am truly thankful they are there.

One of the few positive things my mother did for me was to take the photographs of my life and put them in chronological order in a scrapbook. So many times I have looked at those photographs and so many tales they have told. Using the album has triggered memories because I can "feel" the pictures and, by getting in touch with the feelings, the flashbacks happen. This occurs sometimes with a lot of emotion, sometimes with none. So far, the reason behind the difference is unknown.

My husband's support has been outstanding. He has held me while I cry and shake with anger, awakened me from awful nightmares and shown his respect for me by listening to me when I tell him how I don't like to be treated. This did not come easily and took a lot of work on both our parts. For me, I had to learn to trust his support; to see the difference between betrayal and honest mistakes and blunders. The consistency of his support has given me the opportunity to try to trust. Slowly there is a change coming around. My husband wants my trust very much and so he tries extra hard to stay trustworthy. Remember, he knows betrayal also.

To help with my everyday life and to try to keep on an even keel while going through the different stages of adjusting to being an incest victim, I have been doing volunteer work for various places and causes. It took a while to find the place that suits me best: my local library. Because of my volunteer work, I was offered, and accepted, a part-time position there. Work in a library is something I have wanted since childhood. Even though the work is harder than it appears, I am satisfied. Dreams can, and do, come true. The variety of types of volunteer work that I pick to do has shown me that I can, and do, learn quickly and easily. This last year I realized that I had moved from no self-esteem to low self-esteem. Perhaps the jump to medium self-esteem is not far away.

I don't like the idea that the people who abused me know where I live. I am not afraid that they will hurt me physically, for I know they will not dare. It is the emotional confrontation that I want to avoid. My mother is very good at using a certain technique to emotionally manipulate me. She has only come to our house once, in 1979. She came uninvited and found us on vacation. More work is needed on my part to relax in my own home and to remember that they can only get in if I let them. Since I have no control whatsoever over the comings and goings of my family, being on constant vigil is harmful only to me.

Once I stopped seeing my mother, the guilt I felt left me. My mother is an old, pathetic woman who was abused herself as a child and spent her entire life feeling guilty about it. Myself, I know the guilt does not lie with me. The question I have at this point is: "Did I participate or was I simply trying to survive?" My intellect tells me the latter is true but the rest of me is still confused.

I have worked off a lot of anger by doing yard work and now have a very soothing place to be and see. Plus, doing the upkeep still burns off newly aroused anger. With each new remembrance that occurs, more anger comes out. A good deal of my anger towards my uncle was settled when I had a fantasy about bashing his brains out on the sidewalk of his home. I also had a fantasy about strangling my mother and enjoyed the feeling of her neck as it spilled through my fingers. However, this did not take care of the anger I feel towards her.

Up until this last year I had looked upon my dad as a hero. He was the only one who didn't directly abuse me; the least offensive, so to speak. But I no longer will allow myself to look at him in that light. While he may not have abused me sexually, he never helped me in any way to stop those who were. He just silently turned his back, grew old very fast, and died the day after his fifty-second birthday. My anger towards him is slow in coming to the surface. I know it is there but I am still afraid to get angry at him, afraid to lose a dead man's numbness that I mistook for love.

My brother caused the greatest amount of damage to me in both the emotional and physical sense. Fortunately, if there can really be anything fortunate in being abused, I was not physically injured to any great extent. The humiliation suffered at the hands of my brother is immense and so is the anger that I feel towards him. He harassed me in every way and at any time he could. The harassment didn't have to be sexual to upset me and get the desired results. Realizing that he is also an incest victim helps a little. Thinking about the things he did to me makes me feel anxious with anger.

I try to let the anger out by allowing myself to have dreams where I stab him with a knife. Crying is also a good release for me and something I am able to do with a great deal of feeling. For a while I tried breaking things, but I broke something I liked very much and now regret my course of action. However, I once destroyed a new loaf of bread and found that was good . . . lots of destruction that was easy to clean up and cheap to replace.

Of the many methods I've used during my life to cope with the incest, the ones that have a positive effect on me are the ones that build self-esteem: separation from the perpetrators, counseling, volunteer work and yard work. The negative coping methods — food, drugs, property destruction and denial — lead to self-hatred and no personal growth. In the present stage of my recovery the negative coping methods are still there on my down days but are diminishing. On the up days the positive methods are slowly becoming stronger. With time and work I will learn to live without needing the negative methods. Self-approval is the key to my living a happy life with the incest in its proper place: my past.

While part of me keeps wanting to wonder what I would have been or done had the incest not gotten in my way, I know that this can only cause me anger and frustration. There is no way of knowing. Now I must look at myself the way I am, a 40-year-old woman who sometimes feels 12 and sometimes plus 80. A woman who has gained an enormous amount of control over her once out-of-control life. There is still a lot of work left to do and a lot of sad times to deal with. I struggle with wanting to forget it all again and knowing I will never be able to. My mood swings drive me crazy, but now I know why they are there and how to best deal with the phases of them. To anyone who will listen I will tell my story where once I could not even tell myself. I would not, under any circumstances, trade the pain of today for the pain of yesterday. The pain of healing, while not easy to cope with, is more bearable than the pain of hurt.

Marsha Allen

PROGRESS REPORT ON MARSHA

In my original story, I omitted an important part of my recovery process. Looking back, I can only guess at the reason. I was afraid I was going to fail. So I denied its existence.

I became a volunteer for the Vietnam Veterans of Oregon Memorial Fund. In the beginning of the project, I could have been described as a scared little person. After four years, all of which were far from easy, I emerged a strong, aware, adult woman.

There have been more abuse memories. I was raped as early as age 8, not age 16. Both of my parents abused me sexually and physically. When I was 16, I pointed a loaded shotgun at them. This stopped their active participation in my abuse. For several years my brother prostituted me to sailors and took me to truck stops for the same purpose.

Therapy of some form is essential for me. The women's support group is still a major part of my life. It is a place to regain my balance. At one time I felt resentment at having to "need" therapy. Now I am happy I made that choice. I could be rotting in jail for murder.

INSIGHTS AND PERCEPTIONS

It is a constant struggle to know what is and what is not okay when you have been raised in a dysfunctional family. As you become aware of the reality of your family life, you may find less comprehensible the rules and teachings you have lived by for so many years. Over time you probably invested a great amount of emotional energy in maintaining rules that created faulty thinking. This is very confusing, because while some of the rules are not completely wrong, they are obviously not helping you become who you want to be.

There is a process of becoming aware that the rules you have taken on are not working for you. You need to examine them closely and change what no longer fits. This is no easy task. Something that has been ingrained into your life for so long does not just disappear because you want it to. You have to unlearn dysfunctional thought patterns and then replace them with learning that will help you. Think about the people you associate with and the environment you are in. Look at whether or not they reflect old patterns. If they continue to reinforce the old ways of thinking, maybe now is the time to look at some new ways. Become actively involved in your own reparenting. This is also the perfect opportunity to relearn touch, love, and trust.

BE CHILDLIKE

THE DARKNESS BEFORE THE LIGHT

"If my life really is an unfolding flower
My petals are still very tight. If I
Open up to the incest all the way,
Will my life be worth living?"

Mary-Clare Michna

MY FEELINGS

I scream!
   I scream loud!
       Is this the reason no one likes me?
I scream with hate, anger, and love.
   Sometimes all mixed up.
           But sometimes I just scream
               To let my feelings out.
I scream with confusion
   I scream with fright
       I cry with no reason at all.
Everything builds up in me.
   So I just SCREAM.
           And we let it build up again.
               So I Scream, Scream, SCREAM.

Jody
Age 11

PATTY'S STORY

What I have remembered is that my father sexually abused me throughout my childhood and a sadistic, psychotic housekeeper, Karen, sexually abused and tortured me and my brother. She was in charge of us for a month while my parents were away. As soon as I trusted someone, I tried to tell. My first grade teacher was this person. She told me I would go to a foster home. I became so terrified I wouldn't talk, either to her or the principal who sent for me. This was 1955. I recall standing on the school steps after leaving the principal's office and knowing I had to endure my home, until I could leave as an adult, to take care of myself.

In 1958, just before I was ten, my father became concerned that I was pregnant (I had begun menstruating earlier in the year and had skipped several periods, not an uncommon thing normally for the beginning of menses) and he took me for an illegal abortion in East Los Angeles. The abortionist raped me prior to performing the abortion. My father continued to have sexual relations with me through my teens. My gynecologist prescribed birth control pills to regulate my period which really wasn't irregular, but I began hemorrhaging from the abortion . . . you get the picture?

I filed nearly everything that happened under the category of dream or fantasy. When I was 14 I began keeping daily a detailed and coded journal. I coded the sexual abuse: "I had a bad dream last night I don't remember what it was." As soon as I went to college away from home I began looking for a therapist. I needed not only someone I could trust, but someone who would not be put off by the horrors of the torture the housekeeper performed. When I was 35 I met a therapist who looked like a good possibility. I was seeing her for my infant son's continual screaming. After a year and a half of "checking her out" I decided to see her for myself. My assessment of her was correct.

My father has been dead seven years. I have told my mother most, but not all, the details of my life. She is very spacey and disconnected. In spite of her mental deficiency in certain areas, she has been accepting and supportive; and for the first time we have talked, with her knowing who I really am.

The following are two poems written during the time I began to remember the sexual abuse done to me as a young child. They express my feelings about telling my mother and feelings directed at my father.

Patty

I TOLD MY MOTHER

I told my mother I was molested:
She said I lied.
my face turned black and
my hands beat against my own walls forever.

I told my mother I was molested:
She laughed.
I became a whore and
Searched for a man who could laugh like my mother.
I told my mother I was molested:
She turned her head to the wall and wept large green tears.
My arms fell off to the ground
My private parts withered to scabby bits
My mouth dried up and shut
The earth spun 'round and 'round
And didn't stop once.
I told my mother I was molested:
She kept on making dinner and asked me to make the salad
And set the table.
I set the large black knife at her place
I put poison in the salad dressing
I folded a threat in her napkin
I ran away from home without leaving
And never came back.
I told my mother I was molested:
She fainted dead away.
My eyes rolled back and I saw a snuff movie.
I was the star, I was the audience.
I was the end.

Patty

FATHER'S DAY 1985

Daddy, you bastard
This is your day
I tried to forget it
Forget what you did
Daddy, you bastard, you banged up my life
I'm aching for some kind of clarity, fact
Did you or didn't you fuck with me then?
It feels like you did it again and again.
Well, where was your wife I didn't want me to be?
I was caught in a trap down on my knees
Growing up hungry, growing up lean,
You didn't notice my childhood of screams
Echoing in doorways, refrigerators and cars
Where were your eyes, where was your heart?
Daddy, oh Daddy, you've done it again
Escaped dead — free from the end of my pen
I hope you can hear me way down in the earth
In the concrete bunker that seals in your death
I hope when I stand at your grave and I do
Swearing and crying you'll know it's the truth
Cuz I'm telling you straight
You left me stranded before seven or eight
And now in mid-life for a Father's Day poem
I'm telling you, Daddy,
Don't ever come home.

Patty

PROGRESS REPORT ON PATTY

Recover: I am beginning to know this world after three years of intensive therapy, exclusively devoting my time, minute by minute, and all my thoughts each day towards understanding 18 years of a traumatic childhood.

The process of healing is to re-cover the wounds in a new way. The bandages of trust and safe closeness have to be woven before they bring solace. I was screaming for help and having to reconstruct myself, and weave the bandages all at once.

My therapist and husband understood that abandonment was my greatest terror. They were patient and constant companions, although it was hard for me to acknowledge or even feel that at the time. Those touches evoked all the remembered disappointments, abandonments and betrayals more strongly than the initial telling of the secrets. It seems every step of healing involves another layer of pain. I protest, I rage, but there is no other way. I refuse to choose death and let "them" win.

Now, three years later, I am covering the wounds and this re-covering is done, oh, so differently than the hiding. There are horrendous scars, and things I know I can never do. Sometimes, when I am feeling pretty good, I get a glimpse of those scars and howl with unbearable anguish at what was done to me by my family. I howl at knowing I carry these scars forever.

Recovery: learning every day for the rest of my life how to walk gracefully while carrying a heavy, awkward package that has been sutured to my body.

DECISIONS

Crimson slashes and furtive glances
Streak across the sky.
The ebony sky reflected back to me
Only by the absence of light.

People live out there but I'm
On a child's merry-go-round
With incest memories pushing me in
One direction and a void in another.

If I do make a decision, I'm too
Dizzy to know which direction to go
Sometimes it's like a tile hallway just
Waxed. Too slippery to trust to stand on.

❖ ❖ ❖ ❖

PETALS

If my life really is an unfolding flower
My petals are still very tight. If I
Open up to the incest all the way,
Will my life be worth living?

❖ ❖ ❖ ❖

DEMOLITION

Pain can be sharp and bitter
Impossible to be burdened with.
But it also is a dull throb
In my stomach that never goes
Away even after I'm done crying.

Feeling is so hard sometimes
That it sometimes feels like
Walls would be easier to build
But now that I'm remembering
The bricks and facing my perpetrator,
The walls fall, and the bricks crumble.

✦ ✦ ✦ ✦

FLASHBACKS

The days somehow seem to flow together
To make one continuous dream that is alive
And sucking at me with vicious propensities.
One foot the victim, one in present reality
And me never knowing which way I will fall,
Leaving me . . . confused and disoriented.

✦ ✦ ✦ ✦

A SMALL THOUGHT

Sometimes crying can be soft and as gentle
As a spring rain and leave me feeling sad
Yet happy because tears can heal.

FINDING MYSELF

Hesitantly reaching out to pain,
Feeling guilt, shame, fear, aloneness.
Afraid to be alone, afraid to be afraid.
The thin line of reality and the past
Are too difficult to separate.

Dreams coming uninvited crashing
Through my world and body and
Being exhausted from remembering
And hurting. I feel like I can't
Go on, they just keep coming.

I'm finding it harder and harder
To be in control of what is reality
I'm holding back, so afraid to
Show anger. I have to be quiet
So that I'm violated no more.

The bitter cold of the night dreams
Calls me to join the numbness, to let
The freezing snow swallow my so very
Small self. So peaceful to go quietly
And let go. A struggle not to.
Sometimes I feel or almost hear
The ripping of flesh from my body
So that I can't be hurt again.
In what part of pain will I finally
Find the anger to allow me to go on?

Hold on to me and don't let me go.
Or, if not, just let me go.

❖ ❖ ❖

A SECRET KEPT

Once upon a time there was a
little girl,
Who looked for love and found
hurt,
Who went to her friends and found
rejection,
Who went to God and found
emptiness,
Who looked inside herself and found
humiliation,
Who tried to tell and found
disbelief,
And she grew up to be a Big Girl and found
pain.

Mary-Clare Michna

PROGRESS REPORT ON MARY-CLARE

Healing for me has been a journey of triumphs and despair. The path has not been smooth, nor has it always led me up to the light. Many times the way seemed like a twisted, convoluted tunnel, sometimes toward the light and often away from it. But, my friends and counselors help keep me on the path, even when it seems like I'll never reach the end, and even question why. I listen to them and the child within me, and together we find a way.

Writing, painting, hypnosis and being part of several adult survivors' groups keeps me in touch with my feelings and gives me a way to let go of the feelings and share with others the secrets that held me locked away for so long. Sharing my secrets with others, and hearing theirs, gives me back some of the power I had lost. It also helps me to realize that I am not alone in my journey to recovery. Now all I have to do is reach out a hand and many hands will be there to strengthen me and walk with me on the way to healing. I will reach the light. I won't give up. I am not alone.

CHILD OF THE HOLOCAUST

Stickmen drawn on a cement wall,

Broken teeth broken jaw.

Shadow puppets on the night wall.

Broken legs, the pain in my hip never ceases

Yet we see beauty in everything

We stutter as we talk,

The horrors we have seen

Rape, Incest, and more,

The violent rage of a man who wants me to bleed.

Fortune tossed us a cruel fate, even yet my heart bleeds.

Weeping, weeping, screaming out loud,

We fight on forever more.

Anonymous

PROGRESS REPORT ON THIS AUTHOR

I am writing a great deal these days and have a major poetry reading coming up in January. I have written some major pieces on the German holocaust and have a connection for publication, so the writing comes along well.

I'm at the point myself where I am beginning to become active in doing something to stop abuse and to allow others to know about me and my experiences. The pain that each one of us goes through is eminently understandable by people and that gives me hope! As with victims of the great holocaust, perhaps we can reduce such abuse by its exposure. All I know is that my prayers are for the children and to stop their pain.

STARTING TO HEAL

Sometimes when I think of my past, I think of an unwanted toy in a garbage can. A wound so deep, it will never heal. A broken crystal vase that can never be put back together. A wilted flower. A moldy piece of bread. Something dirty that will never come clean. An unwanted child. A leftover and a left-out.

Now, all that is left inside of me is a really deep scar with the painful memories of a horrible childhood, slowly healing and recovering as a *survivor* of incest for ten years.

❖ ❖ ❖ ❖

There is no apology big enough to cover the scars that were left by an uncaring man or brothers. The holes are too deep to fill. All they can do is heal. But there will always be the memories in there. Now, all I know is that they were responsible for what they did to me. It wasn't my fault at all.

❖ ❖ ❖ ❖

Every once in a while I have a flashback of a part of my past. All of the shame, guilt, and horror of how it felt to be betrayed by the people I love. It will take me a while to trust another man. The men that hurt me scarred me forever. It is so much damage. I am glad I am in counseling now, dealing with it with someone who cares enough to listen to me.

❖ ❖ ❖ ❖

I felt so ugly, inside and out, when I was being abused. I didn't care how I dressed or what I looked like. I would eat a lot to get fat so no one would want me. I often felt like killing myself. I attempted it twice. I tried to cut my wrist with a razor blade. But now, I know that life is worth living and that I am an important person.

Judy
Age 17

FOR FATHER'S DAY

To my dad.

Never been a child

just born

never been a child

just fucked.

Didn't talk too much

just watched a lot

learned a lot.

Wild but tamed

never been little.

But I know how to play the game.

Mom always told me

your dad has needs

I can't meet them all

but you can, so be a good little girl,

He's been through a lot.

Anyway, you got it good.

My pale face mother

stupid white woman.

Powerless bitch.

She gets what she wants by letting others shit on her.

It makes her feel like she's worth something,

and she's been a good wife.

Daddy sure loved her, according to her.

But mom, what about all those other women in his life?

Oh, they're just friends of his, helpless women.

He feels sorry for them and takes care of them.

Most of them are widows.

Not to speak of me, my sisters, their friends and mine.

Great love, a father who takes care of every woman's needs.

Oh mighty fuck, father fuck, oh best fuck of the world, super stud.

Save the Indian race, fuck the chief

never satisfied

had to fuck till it finally fell off.

Cancer you say?

Are you satisfied?

Did you finally come daddy?

I'm tired, leave me alone.

With hate, in rage and anger,
your daughter.
KYOS

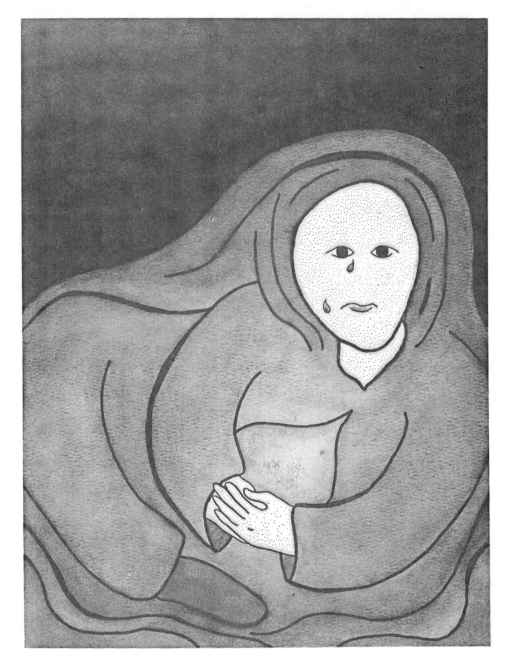

Teresa

LIGHTING UP THE DARK

Journal Entry One

"I Never Told Anyone." In the Forward part of this book, at the very begin-ning, is a question, "Why is it that children who have been molested, sexually abused, or even raped rarely or never tell?" I never told because I did not know for a long time, for many years, that I had been molested. The experience was very clear in my mind. But it wasn't until I was about 14 that I told anyone. That was my mother. For a couple of years before that I carried the guilt and shame.

The day I realized I was molested, from that day on it began growing in me. Before that I knew something had happened that I felt or knew was wrong, was bad, painful, awful. But until I was old enough to know about sex, the whole experience didn't have a name. After I told my mother, I never told anyone. Too, too ashamed. Too angry. Now, no one knows because my mother is dead. I never even put it down on paper until now.

Who will read this? The thought makes me want to stop writing. Tear these pages out but then why? This was never a "pretty" journal. I knew it would never be. I told my mother once outside in the hallway, waiting to go into juvenile court. It might have been a way of saying to her, "I'm sorry, I'm such a rotten kid." I don't know. All I remember is blurting it out. He had raped me. Her father. My grandfather. I expected her to act like a "normal" mother. But she wasn't surprised. She even went on to tell me how she and her sister were raped by him. How she even suspected him of raping other little girls. I don't remember what I felt or thought then. But later I wondered how she could have allowed me to live with the man that raped her. I felt she could have done something to keep me from going through what she went through. But she did nothing. I felt anger.

Journal Entry Two

The little girl peers at the woman with fear-filled eyes. Eyes that say "Don't touch" and "Stay away from me." The woman reaches out her hand to touch her and the little girl runs away holding on to her teddy bear, she runs into a clubhouse. Once inside, the little girl sits upon a makeshift bed. Quietly. Waiting.

Nervously holding her bear tighter and tighter as if she could find safety in her toy animal. Fear is in her eyes and on her face as she sits inside.

What does a child of four or maybe five know about fear? What is fear to this child?

Her grandfather beating her when he comes home drunk, as punishment for an imagined wrong. Her grandfather killing her pet lamb, then cooking it, and eating it, as punishment for talking back at her white step-grandmother in Spanish. Her grandfather staggering through the house drunk, yelling obscenities at her Abuela and her. Her grandfather beating her Abuela. Her grandfather chasing her around his pickup truck as the neighbors stared and laughed.

You can imagine what a spectacle it was. The older man, clad in white Fruit of the Loom shorts, otherwise practically naked, drunk and staggering, yelling, cussing and threatening, "Vas a ver, hija de la chingada" (you'll see, damn you, lil' bitch), with his almost white unruly hair, and chasing an extra short, extra chubby little girl around the pickup truck. As small as she is, the little girl can't run too fast, so you can imagine how drunk he was because he never caught her.

Eventually he lost interest in her, and while he stopped and started arguing with the neighbors that had been looking and laughing over the fence, the little girl ran away. Ran away to her clubhouse, like always, and shut and locked the door. Hugging her teddy bear, her only friend, because she didn't have many friends. Not being allowed to have visitors, because she couldn't make noise because he was either sleeping or sick with a hangover, and if he was woken up he'd get up fighting with her Abuela. Besides their mothers wouldn't allow them to come over because her grandfather was always drunk.

So she'd sit with her stuffed animal in her arms. He'd yell, cuss, and pound the side of the clubhouse with his fists or beat the sides with a pipe or board. He'd get like a madman. A drunk, mad man. Beating and pounding. *Pound. Pound. Pound.* With each pound the little girl withdrew more and more into herself. With each pound her emotions were buried deeper and deeper within, until none surfaced. With each pound her voice was choked and choked, until it was silent. *Pound. Pound. Pound.* It went on.

Until one day the grandfather raped the little girl.

The ultimate punishment for being bad.

The only thing different was that he was sober this time.

Journal Entry Three

"Write. Write about it," her friend and writing teacher tells her.

The young woman sits at her typewriter, at her assigned job as clerk in prison. Pounding away at the keys, feverishly hoping to extract what she had buried inside for so long. *Pound. Pound. Pound.* If only she could make the pounding noise go away, for good, forever. The pounding of her anger. Her rage.

She can no longer run from it. She is no longer the little girl running to her clubhouse. Besides, she is tired of running. Her running has taken her to a string of foster homes, Juvenile Hall, Youth Authority, and finally here.

"She's a scared and hurt girl," her foster parents would say.

"She is out of control," her probation officer said.

"She is a troublemaker, causes more trouble than a hundred Indians on a warpath," the juvenile court judge said.

"She is very withdrawn, a borderline schizophrenic," the psychiatrist wrote.

"She's ba-a-d," her home girls say.

"She's no good, and nothing but a dope fiend," people talked.

"She's a parolee," they say.

"She's an ex-con," they whisper.

She is a young woman, coming face to face with reality, with her life, with the cause of all the pounding that has been going on in her head. She is trying to extract, exorcise all the rotting decay she has accumulated in her life. She is trying to straighten out her life, her mind, her emotions.

"I am angry, and full of rage," the young woman writes in her journal.

She is only trying to find peace of mind by self-expression. She has finally abandoned her clubhouse and has quit running. She is learning to love herself and to face life. In her writing and in her art, she is finding healing.

Pound. Pound. Pound. pound. pound.

Helen

OUR VOICES UNITED

I am very scared
Why me?
I am afraid
What should I do?
Leave me alone
I don't care if you deny it
because it happened and
you *are* a child molester

❖ ❖ ❖ ❖

I made him mad and now he's coming for me
Can I stick it in there?
it will feel good
everyone does it
How could you take your own sister's virginity
you bastard
I hate the sight of you and I always will

❖ ❖ ❖ ❖

Cold and uncomfortable
on the hard floor of the chicken coop
dirty and smelly
and straw in my clothing and hair
Go help your father
I don't want to
Be a good girl
I wish you had died before I was born
so I would never have known you
and I could make you up in my imagination
to be what a good father should be
I'd rather have my imagination
than the reality of you

❖ ❖ ❖ ❖

Your face always hovering over mine
watching my face, watching my face
that was really a turn-on
you said smiling
after you raped me
I want to smash that smile
and be finished with you

❖ ❖ ❖ ❖

Trapped in the bed
no way out
no one to help me
don't please don't
relax . . . doesn't that feel good?
you are sick, very sick
but I won't be part of your illness
you can't make me anymore

Incest Survivors
Rape Crisis Center
Madison, WI

WE SHATTERED THE SILENCE

I remember — gagging from the intense, fast movements
    when he would hold my head
    as he was about to ejaculate during oral sex
looking at the ceiling vent and seeing the sky
    and going outside to it in my mind
the smell of semen all over my body and my mouth
Ray's French-kissing me, and grabbing
    my breasts in the car
my brother, half-laying on me, choking
    me with a black snake: I couldn't breathe:
    I couldn't move — then he raped me
    with the snake, later —
    after he finished choking me.
"They know what is sweet," he said in
    reference to the bugs that were landing
    on my private parts as he
    made me lie exposed before him
"No!" I screamed
"Swallow it, sweet angel,"
"C'mon, you let everyone else do it,"
"If you tell, you will be adopted out."
you have no idea how much you've hurt me,
    and there's nothing you could ever do to

make up for that!

shame on you for taking advantage of a child!

brother, I remember all of it now.

I'd like to slap his face as hard as I could

and tell him about my pain, tell him all the hurt

I endured from him and tell him that I don't

respect him and I don't love him.

Go to hell — and you better not be

hurting the kids. You hurt me —

and I hate you for that —

but don't hurt the children.

I am not keeping silent any longer

I will stop you

I WILL NOT KEEP SILENT ANY LONGER!

Incest Survivors
Rape Crisis Center
Madison, WI

Night Dreams

Shades of gray
blend with early
morning dawn
bringing
confusion,
fear,
and pain.
Beginning levels
of consciousness
hear faint
cries for help.
Wanting to
rescue someone
in distress
I force myself
to
alertness . . .
only to find
the cries
are
mine.

Crystal Ann Jordan

INSIGHTS AND PERCEPTIONS

Feeling the emotions that are intertwined with memories of abuse is the hardest recovery task of all! It demands that you look inside the very core of your being and face your greatest fear — the reality of the abuse. Up until now, your abuse could be denied, stored away, or camouflaged.

When going through the abuse, you were experiencing the spontaneous effect of an intolerable situation. Now the hurt, anger, confusion, hate, humiliation, and a multitude of other feelings continue to reverberate throughout your life. In a way, these emotions keep you in the victim cycle. As these feelings emerge from within, it is healing to allow their expression. They may feel like an underground volcano waiting to erupt, but continuing to stuff them down will not work. You must create some way to vent your feelings, however overwhelming and frightening they may seem. You will feel lighter after releasing some of the intensity.

Do not do this process by yourself. We encourage you to get involved in recovery groups; joining with others who are experiencing similar struggles can be quite freeing.

BE STRONG

TAKING CHARGE

"A new day is dawning for me and I want to be ready."

The Goddess In Me-Diana

JOURNAL ENTRY

The memories come out of the fog of my mind like a hand, trying to choke the creative voice that is in me. With its backaches, headaches, insecurities, gossip, and pressures of life, like fingers it wraps around my newly found voice. Trying to strangle the words that are so eager to be released. Like a hand trying to squeeze the life-giving air from its victim.

I will not submit! I will pick up my pen and write as a victim would pick up a weapon in self-defense. I will struggle to free the unseen fingers that are around me. I must, my life-giving energy is at stake. I must fight to loosen the fingers that are trying to kill my spirit.

I must write and write and write whether or not it makes sense to me. Like the victim fighting for its life I will use whatever resources are within my reach. Since it is my own voice that is at stake I will pick up a well-used pen and my beloved journal to do my battle.

Ryvonne Lewis

TAKING CHARGE

Who is this person locked behind this door?

I feel so numb. I'm just not myself anymore.

I wish that I could turn back the clock.

So that the first time he touched me,

I could make him stop.

For a time I thought there was no one I could tell.

In a way I am glad that he is dead.

For now I am free. Now I know who this person is,

This person is me.

Jean
Age 14

HEALING THERAPY

I am writing about part of the process I have gone through from incest victim to healing survivor. This is reflected in the following chronological excerpts from journals and letters that I wrote throughout my individual and group therapy. I have left the journals mainly in their original voices to preserve and illustrate the many phases, defenses and splits of myself I have come to know, reject, accept and love. These self-masks have been valuable learning tools on my road to greater nurturing and intimacy with myself and others, and also significant indicators of when "my little girl self" is in need.

Although I have completed some major work in therapy, I've discovered much more within myself developmentally that needs reparenting. The recovery from my incest wound continues in my life. This has been a five-year process of waxing and waning through the intimacy struggles I have undergone and conquered as a result of my childhood "and beyond" trauma of incest. I now claim my rightful throne as a survivor of incest.

A new day is dawning for me and I want to be ready. I went to see a therapist, "S.", and poured out as much as anyone can pour out in an hour's time. I gave a brief history of my life, my family, my jobs, and my feelings. S. and I talked about how hard it was for me to be on the other side of the therapist desk. The best thing I liked was that S. thought we could work together on all my issues, for I truly needed a guide. I want to grow and change and know and see where it is I am going and where I've been. It seems this pain is necessary in order to discover the wealth and fun in life that are deep within me bursting to come out. It is the most wonderful feeling in the world not to feel judged, to be accepted for who you are and to be welcomed by another member of the human race.

During the assessment phase of my therapy, S. gave me a test for incest. Most of the questions were very personal and my stomach churned in answering. At the end S. asked me how I felt about the incest test. I told her that it was hard to hear that I had scored *very high* and to hear S. say that I am a victim of incest, overt and covert. That my parents could be the finest people with the finest intentions and no one is to blame; but that the incest is a great cause for my anger and rage: being violated sexually at six to eight years old with enemas at mother's hands. I told S. about mother's cleanliness obsession and that she was known for giving all her younger brothers and sisters enemas. She would also clean my younger cousin out when she stayed with us. I described the red rubber enema bag and the long black insertion tube. While describing the tube I made a circle with my hand. S. saw me do this and asked why I made a circle and what the circle was. I told her I didn't know what my hand meant. I said maybe my subconscious knows, maybe I'll remember at some point.

S. said to go ahead with the "relationship history" homework she gave me to fill out. I took a long time in completing it and in the process discovered a lot about my relationships and how I landed in a net of very destructive ones — many of which re-enacted the ones that I had with my parents. S. asked me how I felt about each relationship, beginning with mine and my mother's. I said I felt like a traitor now, telling the secret.

With dad, I found out I protected him a ton, even when he punched me out when I was a teen, beat me in the breast area and stomach within an inch of my life. My mother intervened, or otherwise I doubt if he would have stopped. S. asked if my mother and dad ever held me in affection. I told about all the "pretend affections" — having to kiss them and all the other relatives good night when I was younger. I realized that, no, there was no affection, ever. I never got anything from them in regard to parenting. The message from them was anger, resentment, criticism and *shame*.

S. asked about any disrespectful sexual attitudes in the home about women and their bodies. I told her that dad was always lifting up my dress as a child to see my underwear. All my uncles did likewise and I got furious always!

My feelings throughout the session were fear and anxiety. I said to S., "Things will probably get more difficult?" S. nodded. It feels good to be able to talk to someone and be so open, knowing you won't be hurt or judged for sharing, but that you'll be asked about your feelings. Sometimes I think I trust too much, have no marked boundary between me and others. There must be distinctions between lost self, found self, self with another.

Maybe I think I've no right to my own body or my emotions because for so long they weren't mine. My body belonged to everyone else. The question is, do I really trust "myself" with S.? Did I ever trust my mother as I was so "enmeshed" with her that I didn't know who I was? Do I need approval from S. or do I constantly strive to be so perfect before her eyes so I can get what I need from her? Good question . . .

In the different arenas of life I've been running from that "enmeshed" feeling. I've never identified it or known what it was. But now I know it's the closing in, the feeling of losing myself in others. It's amazing how much is surfacing that has been buried.

HOMEWORK ON ANGER

This week I'm to begin making note of my anger — notice it, feel it, but don't do anything about it yet.

To get in touch with my feelings of any kind, and most especially anger, I went to a children's bookstore and browsed the shelves awhile. I came away with a couple of books about feelings and self-esteem, *Liking Myself* and *Mouse, Monster and Me*. These books contributed to my search for feelings. I read the anger chapter which correlated anger with "rights being taken away from anyone." They entitled it "Stomping on my Flowers." I felt it rang true — how much it felt like someone stomping on my flowers — the incest wound and mother's devastation of my childlike garden.

I read these made-for-children books faithfully every night and began to think of all the things in my life that I've got anger and rage about, but that lays dormant as the mouse.

Later, in one session, I told S. that I felt mad at her for always asking me what am I feeling. S. wondered if I perceived it as a "demand." I thought not, or otherwise my anger would have been more intense. As it was, I felt plain mad. S. said, "How wonderful you can get mad at me!" I felt her statement to be most strange and out of character . . . in my family no one ever said their feelings, let alone their anger. I'm always afraid of going out of control, like my father did when he beat me up in his fit of rage. To get angry meant you went out of control. I wasn't aware of any other ways, then.

HOMEWORK ON RECEIVING COMPLIMENTS

S. gave me my homework for the week: to receive any compliments I should get and to acknowledge them. I felt really silly doing this.

I thought I'd be able to get back to therapy without anyone giving me a compliment. Then someone at the house complimented me on a good job done on some work. I noticed how I wanted to ignore the compliment, deflect it in some way or say it wasn't true. What are my fears in these intimacy encounters? Someone giving me a compliment doesn't mean necessarily they are crossing my boundaries, but that's what it feels like. I guess they're commenting on something about me they like and I can't handle that yet. It's too close to intimate. I might *owe* them for their compliment. That's what it feels like, owing.

In my family, I was never supposed to hear any compliments. My mother thought I'd grow up to get an "inflated ego." Therefore she kept secret anything nice she ever said about me. It is so ironic that at her wake, when I was a grown woman, a relative told me my mother was proud of me and my vocational work of helping others. I broke down and cried upon hearing this but at the same time wanted to laugh hilariously that I was now hearing the first bit of parental praise through a relative, as I stared at my mother in her coffin.

HOMEWORK: "FUCK-UP CONTRACT"

I made a contract with S. to fuck up, to be imperfect and to shine in my imperfections. All my life, I was the good little, only girl/child in my family. Anything less than perfection was intolerable, so I am embarking upon the journey to be less perfect, less prepared and rehearsed for my one to one sessions with S. and for my group. The danger here was to be perfect about being imperfect. I went that route up and down, round and round until I saw hints and glimmers about what it means to act in spontaneity and not watch my "p's and q's." Some of my dream work at this time clearly illustrated to me how afraid I was of losing control in my life; how intact I needed everything to be, and how to stray from the scheduled was a breach of some secret society that weighed me down.

BOUNDARIES HOMEWORK FROM INCEST GROUP

I discussed the possibility about going to a family wedding and my fears in group today. One member told me she usually would write a set of rules to herself that she looks at while at a family gathering. I found this suggestion most helpful and will use it.

1. You are not to spend the night in the city.
2. You can leave anytime during the evening you want. You do not owe it to anyone to sit in discomfort or emotional abuse or infringement upon your boundaries.
3. You can enjoy tonight for what it is. Practice being with relatives and not becoming enmeshed in their needs and wants.
4. Laughing and dancing are your ways to cope. Enjoy and accept these for what they are. You'll not get your intimacy needs met here.
5. I repeat, you do not need to take care of others here.
6. Take your power.

GRIEVING ANOTHER REMEMBERED ASSAULT

S. asked me what it felt like to be six years old and not very powerful. I related the incident of the garbage man touching me near my vagina when I was six years old. I remember running to mother and she not believing me. S. asked me how I felt. Sad, I said. Then I continued to give some excuses as to why mother didn't protect me. S. said if I weren't still "caretaking" mother then I'd have to feel the full force of my sadness. I told S. there weren't any more tears left. She said there are many more tears; my little girl needed protecting and no one was there to protect and care for her. How very sad; I felt in utter agony as the session closed. S. said it'd be very painful talking to my little girl, going all the way back to talk and tend to the little girl inside me. S. suggested I'd been a little adult all my childhood, out of survival, because of my family system and the incestuous violations.

My homework for the week is to find a six-year-old girl, follow her around, feel and experience what it's like to be six years old. Also, to write a letter to my little girl telling what I needed and wanted.

I asked S. how long my little girl would be around with me (as I felt one-tenth of the feelings that lay dormant within me). S. said "Forever." I told S. I imagined my little girl locked away in the attic in chains. The session ended.

LETTER TO MY LITTLE GIRL
(Variation on *Little Boy Blue)*

Little girl sad

Come tell me your wounds

Sheep in the meadows, cows in the corn

Where is my six year old who looks after me

She's under the haystack fast asleep.

Will you wake her? No, not I.

For if I do, she's sure to cry.

RECYCLING LETTER TO MOTHER

Dear Peaceful Recycling Mother,

I have been giving much thought to this letter and decision before I've written it to you. I know my decision is inevitable. I have decided to leave you. If I could, I would not choose my same family, my same dad, and not even my same mother. My feelings about this are that I'm changing drastically inside. I can't completely define it or know what's happened. But, I feel it, nevertheless, and that makes it valid.

You see, mother, I've come to know about and feel what it means to be nurtured, through words, through hugs, both definitely foreign concepts to me. They were a void in my life, something I felt I had no right to. Because I've been in such pain about the incest from you and dad, I've truly been searching for a better way. This better way is asking more of me than I dared it would when I started out, but my insides tell me that it is the best thing in the world for me, and my best interests are in mind.

As much as I hate and deplore what you've done to me, mother, you have given me some gifts. That wasn't enough because the biggest unhealthy part of you didn't show me how to live life; instead you showed me how to die because you wanted to die. I want to blame you for that, mother, because that is how we acted in our family. But, I've come to realize that you couldn't give what you didn't have.

I told myself, dear mother, that I would never have a child until I thought I was okay "emotionally." I haven't felt okay most of my life. I've never had a child and I'm not sure if I ever want to. That doesn't matter as I believe in other kinds of motherhood — to the children and people I know. It's called nurturing. Because of my deprivation, I feel awkward in it yet. I know now it can get better as I practice and practice. Good-bye, Mother.

Love,

D.

THINKING ABOUT A SESSION WITH FATHER

I told S. what dad said the other week about wanting a key to my house to bring some fish by, and how I had cringed. The whole thing felt so incestuous to me, him coming by invading my house. Even though dad was never overtly incestuous with me, he more or less continued his covert innuendos and at times treated me like his girlfriend instead of his daughter. I hated that. I told S. the thought of a session with dad felt unimaginable at this time. I told S. all I was concerned about was finding out *was Mother truly emotionally ill?* S. said she doesn't need to know, that she already knows she was. The task is to talk to your dad about this when you're ready. How do I prepare? S. asked what I wanted to tell my dad. I didn't really know at that moment. She asked me to make a list of what I want and don't want from him and then offered her presence at the session. I felt safety in that. I will shove this away for a while now.

Dad is pressuring me to go to Florida or Italy with him. He's coming on with the, "Poor me, no one to do things with." A friend of his asked him the other day if he was married. He told me he should have said, "Yes, I'm married to my daughter." Then in my rage I became fuming, silent, and thought, "how sick." I need to get mad at him. I felt like Scarlett O'Hara: "Tomorrow, tomorrow."

THERAPY SESSION WITH MY FATHER AND S.

My father agreed to come to a one-to-one session with me. I felt surprised and, most of all, fearful. In group, I talked at length about the list of things I wanted and needed to tell my father. The list went something like this:

1. My motives for coming to therapy.
2. My pain and shame about the incest with mother.
3. My pain and shame about the covert incest with father.
4. My sadness and anger about having a father who was gone most of my childhood.
5. My shame and rage about being beaten up by my father and my fears of him since then.
6. My rage that he didn't protect me from mother's incestuous behavior.
7. My rage about father's acceptance of boys in his life, but never a daughter.
8. My feelings about being cheated that my father treated me like a girlfriend instead of a daughter.
9. My rage about the demeaning way father talks about women and acts towards them.
10. My rage about father's boundary infringement (i.e., wanting a key to my house, etc.).
11. My rage about touch deprivation from him. The only thing he ever did was wrestle with me when I was a child.
12. My feelings of distrust with him when he would give things instead of nurturing.

In group, I vented my rage and fears of him and got the support I needed in doing this session with him.

I was very nervous when father appeared. I introduced him to S. and we all sat down. S. began the session with some introductory remarks and some overall rules about the session. Then the whole thing was in my corner. My voice was shaking and I knew I could rely on my list, but once I got started saying the first few things I needed to tell him, the rest flowed fast and furious. It was completely unexpected when he denied beating me up as a teen. I didn't think he'd actually deny this. It's funny, he didn't really deny any of the other behaviors I listed for him, but he was really angry when I confronted him on beating me up. As for his part in my incest with mother, he deflected that one pretty well, saying that he didn't know about any of it. He didn't know when mother was emotionally ill. S. saw he was interrupting my process and stopped him, asking him to wait till I was done to respond. He did not like S. telling him what to do. I felt S. in my corner and felt protected by her. I was still scared of his violent nature, yet I felt more powerful than I had ever been with him in my life.

In ending the session I set up some boundaries about not seeing father too often because I don't get what I need from him. He agreed to this and said in the session that he loved me and wanted my happiness, regardless of what has happened. He said he never wanted "all this brought up again." I didn't agree to that, as that would limit my freedom. The session ended and S. thanked my father for coming. My father and I went to coffee for a short time. What I learned most of all was that my father didn't need me to take care of him anymore. He took care of himself so well in the session. I felt assertive and powerful that my father now knew my rules and the limits of our relationship. The only important thing for me was that I spoke out.

HYPNOSIS: GROUP SESSION

Last night S. led us into a creative visualization. We began by relaxing each part of our bodies and each time S. would say, "Know you have a choice."

Then S. suggested we imagine a beautiful scene in which we were enjoying everything in it.

Then, step by step, we descended to a cave where there was a huge mirror with cracks in it. One by one different characters, or splits of ourselves, came out of the mirror and talked to us.

There was the tough little bully who had a lot of defenses to protect himself.

S. suggested he didn't need to be so defensive anymore to get his needs met. The little bully could even survive love!

There was the little baby (I got a headache here) crawling around looking to be cared for.

Green Woman appeared and acted out awhile and then learned she didn't need to be jealous to get her needs met anymore. She learned she could get all the love and attention she wanted.

The Frozen Woman appeared and was invited to "not numb out" anymore. She could receive all the deserved nurturing people wanted to give to her.

During the visualization, when the different characters were coming and going, I realized that close up they were me, and I began to melt into them. When we got to the shame part, we were to imagine shame. Mine was "icky" black and green, bulky slime, and I purged it with a dentist's suction cup. Then S. suggested we toss it onto the meadow-land. At first I didn't want to, because it was so horrible, but then I thought it'd make good compost.

For me, it was hardest to go down the stairs into the cave and as much as I trusted S. and wanted to be open to the experience, I knew I needed my survival kit of food, candle and Swiss army knife.

This type of trance was very relaxing and powerful. The "nurturing Mother" who came out at the end embodied everything I never got, and modeled everything I could now learn and needed to know to give this nurturing to myself.

HOMEWORK ON JEALOUSY
(What I learned in my family about how people show they care for each other)
1. They leave, go far away = father gone in my childhood.
2. They watch, stifle and possess = mother possessed my body and soul.
3. They go past my boundaries = both my parents.
4. They go crazy with their emotions = mother's side especially (shock treatments, illness, fights at weddings).
5. They don't talk or show any feelings, only silence and pretense.
6. They give material things rather than nurturing.
7. They shame, put down, criticize and judge personhood.
8. They never touch, except exploitatively.
9. They preach perfection.
10. They deny.
11. They push their values on me.

12. They preach right and wrong, good and bad.

13. They keep many secrets.

NIGHTMARE

Last night I woke myself up with a scream. The nightmare was about my mother sexually abusing me. Mother was there in the dream writing sexual notes to me which I couldn't believe. There were vivid sexual connotations going on and some movie dream script which denoted sex with daughter. As I watched this take place it was so unbelievable. This was the moment in the dream when the lens came in close to see who was the victim of the sexual abuse. It was not some middle-aged woman, but a tiny precious little six-year-old girl. She was Me, as photographed as a child. It was a shock to see the truth. I tried to get away and scream. I opened my mouth and nothing came out. I couldn't get away from my mother at all — she was everywhere.

THE BODY REMEMBERS

Today I went to a physical exam with my doctor. She was very gentle and understanding. I was okay when she began but immediately when she started the rectal exam I felt like sobbing and I actually started to cry. I knew my body was remembering my incest with mother, all the enemas from six to eight years old that my body's cells don't forget. I felt somewhat surprised at my body's immediate reaction to this exam because I have had physical exams throughout the years without such reactions. I felt encouraged that my body at least immediately reacted to the rectal and that I refused to get traumatized or hold anything in. My body has come a long way.

Today after the rectal exam I knew the reality: that the incest happened. Regardless of mother's intentions, it was abusive and destructive to my young life, and it is taking a lifetime to heal. There is a big difference now than before. I can trust my body — it knows and remembers.

I am made whole. I deserve all my parts. I have felt deficiency too long. I am not meant for separateness from myself and others. I now realize I deserve the life I never knew, or knew only in glimpses or nuances. I want to be bold and cleansed from clogged pathways of my mind's denials and untruths. I want to be free to be me, to love myself and be loved.

The Goddess In Me–Diana

ROGRESS REPORT ON DIANA

I am a 46-year-old, working class woman, who has been healing from the trauma of incest. I first discovered I was an incest victim at the age of 41. I first came to therapy because of recurring nightmares. All of this is a splendid and miraculous journey, filled with all the pain I could not feel at age six.

Each piece of therapy has been vital: incest, sexuality, reparenting, anger, abuse group, couples. All has led to reclaiming lost parts of myself, which I disowned by numbing out. I did extra work through journalizing dreams, to go even deeper into parts of myself, to uncover secrets of my little six-year-old, held close. In my journey I have learned about trusting my intuitive self, and that she is my safest self to whom I can turn any time. I am confident that I will continue to speak and listen to my little one and nurture her through her fears so our life can explode with joy, tenderness and self-intimacy.

I am grateful for all the expert guides in the forms of spirits, therapists, dreams, nature and the Great Mother Goddess herself. Special gratitude and love to Astrid Elsora Bergie who helped me with this piece. My love in forgiveness to my earthly mother who so needed to give her little one everything I'm giving mine now. The most gratitude and love to "Little and Big Diana" who has gradually opened her heart to the healing process. To the two internally discovered families who have helped me discover how paying attention to self-needs relieves abuse.

KATHLEEN'S STORY

My father battered my mother until his death in 1973, after a 30-year marriage. Because she had no power over my father, my mother took her anger and frustration out on my sisters and myself in the form of physical and mental abuse.

At the age of six I was sexually assaulted by a neighbor, a man I felt I could trust. As a child I had always been considered a "cutie" by just about every man I came in contact with. Therefore, when the assault happened, I felt it was my fault. Subconsciously, I began an effort to become as sexually undesirable as possible. By age eight I was grossly overweight. I had been reed-thin until that time. I felt that being overweight would keep me safe.

I have two sisters. One is 12 years older and the other is just 12 months younger. My birth was an attempt to save my parents' marriage. My younger sister's birth was a last-ditch effort for a male child. As a result of the war zone in which I was being raised, I was never a child. I became my younger sister's mother and my older sister's best friend and confidant. I also played with Barbie Dolls until I was in the sixth grade. I took quite a bit of ribbing for this, but it was the only way I could fantasize how normal family life could be.

The years that followed contained more episodes of assault by men. I had by now a built-in defense mechanism (also subconscious) to control these situations. It still didn't help me from being permanently scarred, but now I realize I am a very strong and creative person, having survived it all.

All my life I have wanted and needed a child. Someone to mold, shape, teach, nurture and love in ways I never was. The first step was to find a new man. A man I could trust, who would understand at least some of what happened to me. A man who would be genuinely appalled that such things could happen to anyone. Secondly, I had to conquer the fear that if I had a child I would not repeat the kind of parenting that I had experienced.

Well, I found a good man (there are a few left), and after a seven-year battle with my fears of becoming a poor and abusive parent, I gave birth last August to a beautiful daughter. You'd think my troubles are over, but they've begun again.

Men are attracted to my daughter much the same as they were to me. I need to teach my daughter so many things. I need to equip her with so many skills, so she can have the power I never thought I had. But I have to do it in a loving way so she will not be the wreck I have been at times. At this very moment as I write this story, I am shaking from head to foot and I have developed a headache from recounting the memories.

I don't think these memories will ever fade, but now I try to help other victims. I hope to someday pass my torch along to my daughter. I hope she can accept it. We are each other's legacy.

Kathleen Kelly

PROGRESS REPORT ON KATHLEEN

I am currently in my fifth year of employment at a sexual assault and domestic violence crisis center. When I am not being paid for my efforts, I volunteer my time on our 24-hour crisis-intervention hotline. I do not believe that total healing is possible; however, I do absolutely believe that you can go on and make a difference as you do.

I go forward in my daughter's name. My daughter is now 3 years old, and continues to be a source of total joy to me.

I do not foresee a time when I am not involved in this cause, whether I am employed or volunteering. As a result of my victimization and subsequent realization of it, I can never not participate in the recovery process of others. I am fine, and I will continue to be fine. I am a stronger person for having endured.

THE ODOR OF TRUTH

The following poem was written by my 23-year-old daughter after entering therapy. She was a victim of years of sexual, physical, and emotional abuse.

I was also a victim of the same type of abuse. Sharla and I have grown together and learned a lot of lessons most people live their lives without having to think about. But we have survived!

My life has a new odor

It has more truth.

Truth —

The truth they say, is one's ultimate power.

I never knew the truth therefore, I never knew the

power. Oh yes, I had power, ruling, bitchy, domineering,

destructive power.

But that's not what they were

talking about.

I still slip into the old power, the useless power.

But now I'm learning the truth. It's not always nice.

But reality stinks now and then.

Now there is a new odor. The odor of truth, and it's

as refreshing as the air after a good, hard rain in

the spring. It washes the earth fresh, new and clean.

I still stink now and then but mostly I feel like

the earth after a good hard rain.

Sharla K. Smith

INSIGHTS AND PERCEPTIONS

There is something strong, hopeful, and freeing about reclaiming the power that was taken from you. Inner strength develops when you gather back what once was stolen and lost. It is difficult to take charge of your life when you have never had that opportunity. You may stumble and fall while trying out your own wings, but that is how you learn to fly. Some ways to reclaim your power might be to: 1) write a letter to the offender(s) telling them your feelings about the abuse, 2) share with a member of your family what happened, 3) get involved in an organization that is helping others heal, 4) take a class in self-defense, 5) learn to exercise your rights by taking assertiveness training, 6) do something you have always wanted to do and never had the courage to do. This list could go on and on. Find actions to take that will help you feel strong and in control.

It is time to realize you have choices all around you. Acknowledge that this is your life and you can choose to create life the way you want it to be.

BE POWERFUL

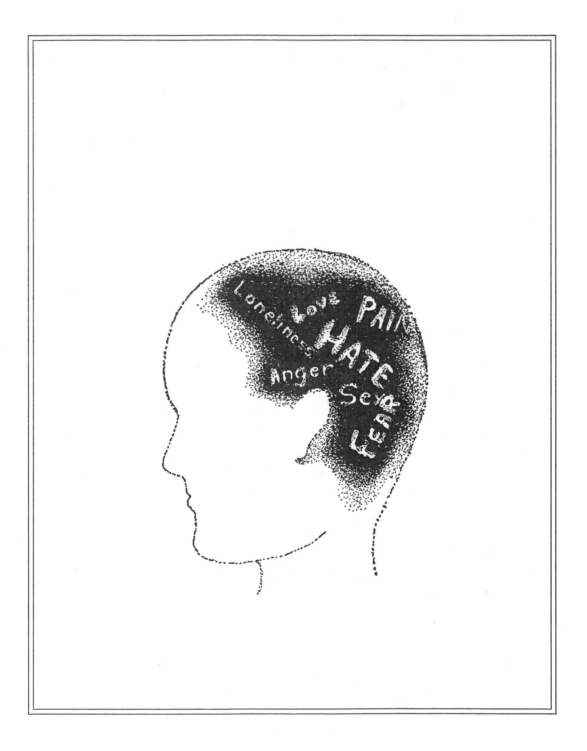

CHAPTER ELEVEN

FINDING A VOICE

"There's an incredible feeling of wanting to run — of wanting to be busy with other things — yet knowing that only by talking about IT will the fears and hurt go away."

Jill

TELLING ABOUT IT

You stumble on words a lot and your thoughts ramble.
You stutter and your stomach feels like
    you want to throw up
You forget to end sentences — forget to breathe —
    and you talk real fast, trying to make your words
    keep up with your mind — until you say a word
    that sticks in your throat —
        and fear takes over
and your mind goes numb and you mumble some more
    wishing you never even began talking
        about IT.
    All of your fears still connected
    and you wonder who you can trust.

But still,
       words keep coming out of your mouth.
There's this unexplainable feeling
       that if you don't tell right NOW
       you'll never again tell anyone
           about *IT*.
Your body hurts where you hurt as a child
and you wonder why the bruises and cuts
don't show on the outside when you can
feel them all so painfully inside.
       You start remembering and telling about things
           you thought you had forgotten
The nightmares start up again
       and sleeping with a light on becomes comforting.
You feel sad — frustrated — confused — guilty —
         disgusted — victimized — depressed
           and angry.
You yell a lot and you cry. You throw things
and you hit a lot of pillows, screaming out your hurt —
     or,
you curl into a small ball;
       your throat tightens, and your fear
is so overwhelming, that all you can do is whisper
There's an incredible feeling of wanting to run —
       of wanting to be busy with other things —
          yet knowing that only by talking
             about *IT*
       will your fears and hurt go away.
So, you keep telling
You realize you can't deny
       what happenend any longer. *IT's* a part of who you are,
of why you respond the way you do
         to love and touch.

IT becomes a part of what makes you unique
     and also part of your strength;
     as the realization comes that
     you are not a frightened child — hurt and unsure —
          but an adult — capable and strong.
You know how and when you want to say "NO,"
          and when you want to say "YES."
Then you take some deep breaths and try to relax,
     because you know that telling
          about *IT*
        will be easier the next time.

Jill

PROGRESS REPORT ON JILL

For years, I have been learning to get in touch with my anger over being sexually abused. I beat pillows — I screamed and cried. But not until I could get beyond the anger and forgive those who abused me did I experience any inner feeling. Though it didn't come easily, I was able not only to have forgiveness for them, but to truly love them.

At this time in my life, through my church, I am working with teenage girls who have drug- and alcohol-related problems. I am co-facilitating an ongoing support group for women who were sexually abused as children. We offer them hope and healing through prayer and encouragement.

In the future, I am working towards establishing an ongoing support and information group for teenage girls who have been sexually and physically abused.

RELEASE

There is a

Scream

Welling up inside of me

"Let Me Out!"

"Let Me Out!"

It says.

But I don't know how!

It wants to come out in sound

And in action

Tearing, breaking, hitting, throwing

Any way possible

Just to come out.

But until it does

There will be the

Sickness

Deep, deep inside

Won't you help me to speak,

Please?

Rylee Brown

I WAS 25 AND A CHILD

Some women are fortunate enough to know at an early age that their family is different. But not I. Not until years of trying to fit into a strange mold, years of non-affection, years of unhappiness — trying to figure out what it was about *me* that was so wrong. After a year of professional analysis I found out the truth — that it was they who were strange and not I.

All of my life I have been an intelligent, capable, strong and lovable woman who experienced time and again empty and abusive relationships with men. I felt no inner courage when faced with job challenges. I solved problems by running. I was frightened when I left the security of my room, felt claustrophobic in crowds, agoraphobic on a deserted beach. I never strayed too far from the nearest bathroom. I felt like a maniac in the presence of a man. I was never satisfied or happy just to be alive.

In a rare moment of intimacy my mother shared the circumstances of my birth. Picture a maternity home in the late '40s; a midwife and a country doctor are present. My father is in the room. My mother is 18 years old and totally ignorant of the birthing process. It must have been the transition phase of labor when the pains are most intense and the emotional toll was the greatest as she began to scream in terror that she was going to die. My father ran out of the room. The doctor administered ether and soon I was born.

Born into a world of screams and anger for causing such pain. There was no warm welcoming committee for me. My earliest memories are of loneliness, searching for affection and warmth and looking for smiles of approval. I received instead messages of, "It would certainly be easier for us if you did not exist. Do this or do that for us. Stay out of the way. Be quiet. Do not make any demands." In essence, "Do not exist."

No wonder I found it difficult, if not impossible, to build a positive self-image. No wonder that I jumped with instant adulation toward anyone who would show me the least amount of attention or affection without knowing whether it was healthy or not. I only knew that it was attention and that it felt good, almost narcotic.

How ready I was for a Catholic priest to bestow his graces of attention, recognition, and physical affection. I was twelve and a half years of age and so desperately lonely and starving for affection. During a rehearsal for a May crowning of the Virgin Mary, he caught my eye and mouthed the words, "I love you." I blinked my eyes, so sure was I that I was seeing a vision. He repeated the words, "I love you." Then he dismissed the group. I was the last to leave. He grabbed me and hugged me and tried to kiss me. God, I thought, this man loves me. I was overwhelmed with a rush of feelings that I cannot even now label. I rushed out of the room, my heart racing. Since no parents were at the rehearsal he drove us all home, leaving me as the last one to deliver. After insisting I sit next to him in the car, he pulled me over to the middle of the front seat. Before I could protest, his hand was between my legs and fumbling for my vagina.

Thus began 13 years of weekly molestation by a respected and powerful man who was a Catholic priest in a quiet Midwestern farming community. I was betrayed by an adult man that I trusted.

The incredibly devious and subtle way in which he manipulated his way into our family was indeed criminal. Into the midst of rural poverty and social ignorance he brought gifts of clothing, food, and trips to movies, concerts and plays. He skillfully orchestrated situations in which he could, unobserved, fondle and touch, manipulate and caress the sexual organs of all the girls in my household.

After many months of agonizing fear and almost paralyzing aloneness, I left home and the clutches of this priest who was rapidly suffocating me.

I was 25 and a child. I bounced from relationship to relationship, leaving each one after being emotionally drained to nothingness. Into my emotional desert came a flood of anger that decimated what was left of my spirit. The self-destructive nature of my anger alerted me to seek professional help. I learned that many victims of childhood sexual molestation follow a pattern throughout their lives. My life seemed to be a carbon copy of that pattern. My rage manifested itself in flight behavior, unsuccessful relationships with men, excessive use of drugs and alcohol, compulsive eating, inexplicable outbursts of anxiety and anger, abysmally low self-esteem, and very little self-confidence.

Through the fine expertise of one woman counselor, I began to raise some serious questions. Why was I so susceptible at twelve and a half years of age? Why did I feel so powerless to fight off the molestations of a priest? Why did I feel so responsible for the disease that infected me and my whole family?

Through the painful dredging of buried memories I discovered I had been sexually molested by two male cousins when I was six years of age, that I had been sexually molested in elementary school by older boys, that I had been sexually molested by my own grandfather as early as five years of age. A shocking and lonely truth blasted my present reality. My own mother had been aware of my sexual molestation by my cousins. Both her behavior toward me and also her attitude, then and now, implied that she blamed me. Why did my mother not protect me? Was she also a victim of childhood sexual molestation? Had she internalized the feelings that women were to be used by men for whatever purpose whenever they chose? Was she too frightened to speak out? Would anyone have listened? After the birth of my sister in the late '50s, my mother suffered an overwhelming depression. She sought help in a sanitarium in which her only treatment was electric shock.

Unbeknownst to me, I had been suffering both her pain and also my own for all those years. Had she been able to solve her own victimization as a child, she would not have carried it over to me by being over-protective, acting like a doormat, and being silent when she saw someone abusing her own daughter. It was no wonder that I was almost catatonic with rage.

Curiosity led me to inquire into the whereabouts of the priest who sexually molested me and my sisters. Imagine the feelings I had when I discovered he was not dead, that he hadn't resigned or retired. Rather he was alive and well and functioning as a Catholic priest in another Midwestern farming town.

In April of 1985 I reported him to his Archbishop. The following is the letter that I sent:

Dear Archbishop,

My name is ____. I am currently involved in a therapy/support group for women who have been molested as children. I was molested by a Catholic priest when I was 13 years of age. This priest is currently functioning in your archdiocese. His name is ____ and he is the pastor of ____ Parish. I am very concerned because I fear he may be molesting children and/or women today.

To document further: From July 1960 until fall 1972, ____ sexually molested me at these locations: at rest areas along various highways and in movie theaters across the state.

During my high school years of 1960 to 1964, ____ molested me weekly in the kitchen of my parents' home (under the pretense of helping me with my homework), on the way to music lessons, in the Catholic church choir loft and attic, and in the Catholic grade school.

Isolated incidents occurred in my bedroom and in my parents' home (while it was being painted with paint _____ had purchased for the project), in the rectory, in the basement of the grade school, and in a motel room in Canada.

I am reporting this to you, not to press charges against this priest but to inform you that he has in the past molested me and my sisters and may be molesting someone today. I would like to save one person from the emotional and spiritual pain that I have suffered for the last 20 years.

My family was incredibly poor and socially isolated. There were ten children on a struggling farm. He took advantage of our extreme poverty and of the naiveté and social ignorance of my parents. We were flattered, proud, and felt blessed that a Catholic priest of God was visiting our home and showering us with gifts, praise and attention.

Our parish needed a choir director and an organist. _____ offered to pay for my music lessons, which afforded him the opportunity to have me alone with him weekly. To further ease the financial burden of my parents, he bought clothes, shoes, and birthday presents for my brothers and sisters. He paid for most of my college education and bought me clothes and cars.

Throughout this time period there were countless opportunities for him to be alone with me or my younger sisters, and he was often dressed as a priest representing God and His Holy Church. He would say such things as, "It's okay, I'm not going to hurt you. I'm a priest. I'll teach you about these things. I love you."

After struggling for years to break away from the powerful dependency trap I was in, I left home in 1973, at which time _____ increased his molestations of my sisters.

My parents, by this time fearful, inadequate, confused, and aware of the betrayal of a priest they had once respected and trusted, tried to break off all contact with _____. In a fit of alcoholic anger, he publicly embarrassed them from the pulpit. He shamed and insulted them in front of the whole congregation, forcing my mother to leave the service in tears. Still faithful, however, my parents joined another Catholic church in the area.

I have prayed and sought much counsel in the preparation of this letter. Had I found out that _____ was not alive, or was retired and receiving extensive help

for his problems, I would not have sought your help in this matter. The fact that
he is functioning today as a priest and as a representative of the Catholic church
bothers me a great deal.

Please investigate this matter and respond.

*Editor's note: Several letters have been exchanged between this author and the Arch-
bishop. His last letter to her stated: "I can tell you that I spoke with _____. He assures
me that nothing of this nature has happened since the times indicated in your letter. Also,
there is no evidence whatsoever to indicate that there has been a problem these past years.
I believe _____ is telling the truth. As you may surmise, he is approaching the age of re-
tirement. He will be seventy years old shortly. I hope the above information puts your
mind at rest."*

*After receiving this letter the author wrote a letter to her offender which reads as
follows (with a few deletions of repetitive material):*

Dear _____,

As I collect my thoughts to write this letter to you, I am bombarded with so
many different thoughts and feelings that I find it almost impossible to put into
words what I am now feeling and thinking about what happened to me beginning the summer of my thirteenth year.

By now you know that I have reported you to your Archbishop. You sexually
molested me for 13 years until I left home in 1972. I am only writing to you now
because this is one more step that I must and want to take in my own healing
process.

The emotional and physical trauma that I felt as a child can be compared to
the physical and emotional trauma felt by some Vietnam War Vets who are now
experiencing the affects of war and Agent Orange on their spirits and on their
bodies. Like the various forms of cancer showing up in their bodies, so too the
trauma of your abuse has taken its toll on me and my whole life, up to and
including this time, even today as I write this letter.

I trusted you, a priest, a man of God. I idolized you and your dynamic
charisma that seemed to be doing so much good for people, the Church and for
God! You were 30 years older than I! How could you use your hand, anointed
with Holy Oil, to fondle and caress my breasts, to manipulate and to masturbate
my vagina? How can you justify that behavior with your vocation as a priest of
the Holy Roman Catholic Church?

I was not the only child you molested. My sisters have come forth to acknowledge your attempts and successes. There were others outside my family.

How could you ever imagine that you were doing me or any child a favor by sexually molesting us? Sexual molestation is legally defined as any sexual contact with a child or the use of a child for the sexual gratification of someone else. It includes the fondling of the genitals, or asking the child to do so, oral sex and attempts to penetrate the vagina or anus.

You, and your sick tendency to seek intimate, nonjudgmental, affectionate relationships with children have nearly ruined my whole life! I trusted you and you violated that trust! Never since that time have I been able to form a lasting, healthy, trusting relationship with a man. During the most formative years of my life, when I should have been forming healthy, normal attitudes about my own sexuality, you chose to "teach me about sex" by forcing me to masturbate you, by manipulating me into situations where you could sexually molest me, by using bribery and friendship to get me to sexually satisfy you, and by using threats to enforce secrecy. I was so afraid then, and so concerned to protect my parents, my brothers and sisters, and to protect you, that I allowed this abuse to continue for so long.

You sensed a weakness in our family structure, you knew my parents were poor and socially backward, timid, and in awe of you. *You took advantage of this! You molested me and my sisters! And you lied about it!*

For your own purposes you planted in me the seeds of open rebellion, hatred, and distrust of my own parents — the only people who could have helped me, had they known the truth.

So many physical and emotional side-effects are still with me — my fear of closed-in areas, my fear of large luxury model cars, my fear of men, my anxiety attacks, my agoraphobia . . . I have not been able to sing for over ten years or sit and play the piano. I have the paralyzing fear that someone will come up from behind me and molest me as I sit down to practice.

You did me no favors by buying me clothes, music lessons, college or cars. You took away my childhood and my adolescence. You molested me when I was powerless to defend myself.

Within two weeks of receiving this letter, I want you to write a formal letter of apology signed by yourself and witnessed by your Archbishop. I want you to address this letter to my family and in it to apologize for the damage you inflicted on me and them. I want you to seek professional help for yourself.

In conclusion, I want to call your attention to Matthew 18: 6 and 10. "But whoso shall offend one of these little ones which believe in Me, it were better for him that a millstone were hanged about his neck, and that he were drowned to the depths of the sea."

Editor's note: This letter was sent in December, 1985, and as of yet the author has received no response.

I am now 39 and an adolescent. I am piecing together a new life based on the knowledge that I am truly lovable, capable and strong. Knowing the truth has helped to set me free from my paralyzing past. I am learning how to trust, how to think, how to feel and how to assert my rights.

Anonymous

PROGRESS REPORT ON THIS AUTHOR

I searched for and found a feminist attorney who helped me to compose a demand letter and to sue the Catholic priest for damages. After six to nine months of long-distance correspondence she and I succeeded in demanding and obtaining a sum of money from him!! This sum in no way compensates for the years of delayed stress from his sexual assault but it gave me a feeling of closure to nearly three years of individual and group therapy.

Breaking the silence about his molestation of me, and my reporting him to the Child Abuse Registry as well as to his archbishop, and my demanding some restitution through a legal channel, has helped me to reclaim my sense of power.

Three more steps that I want to add to my present recovery process include:

1. To mend my spirituality, by finding a spiritual community.
2. To lose the weight of fat and "anger" my body carries.
3. To join a mixed support group.

NAMING

there are things that need to be given a name
there are shadows that need to be given faces
there are touches
                caresses
                probing tongues

it is time for naming
cool saliva oozing from a mouth
cool saliva trailing into her
cool saliva, wet on her skin
                        cold on her skin
                        chilling her in the night air
sweaty hands
hot hands
skin sticking to skin
sweaty hands tugging at her pajama bottoms
sweaty hands grabbing her into stillness
sweaty hands pressing the screams back into her mouth
and
        then
                there
                    was
                        the numbness that poured like blood
                        that pushed the air out of her
                        that pushed the air out of her hips
                                out of her legs
                                out of her fingers
that pushed the names out of her mind
that pushed away the weight of his body on hers
that pushed away the weight of his grown body on her still child-form

IT IS TIME FOR NAMING
the shadow that slithered into her room
                           haunted her closet and under her bed
                           and burrowed into her eyes
        the shadow had hot sweaty hands
        the shadow had hot sweaty hands
              that pulled her night clothes off
              that felt all over her body
              that groped all over her body
the shadow has hands
the shadow had a coldness about the rest of him
    his lips were cold
              the only thing that came from those lips
              was
              slimy wetness
              spit
              tongue
                  in her
                  in her mouth
                  in her ear
                  in her vagina
                  in her
the shadow had a tongue

the shadow lay heavy upon her
the shadow ground into her
      sometimes she thought she would never walk again
the shadow groaned, panted and collapsed on her
the shadow lay heavy upon her

in the daylight the shadow was nearly unrecognizable
           the child could scarcely remember
           and when he dressed her for school,
           his hands were cool and dry
and when the child went to school
the shadow loomed over her

but no one saw
instead they said, "behavior problem"
                    "not working up to ability"
                    "depressed"
and when the child went to church
the shadow loomed over her
            and she said Hail Mary and
                Our Father
                and still felt unclean
the shadow loomed over her
                        even in the daylight
                        even in the church
the shàdow loomed over her
even when she was no longer a child

and when she tried to speak to it
        she said things like, "I want to die"
                and, "I'm so sorry"
                and, "How stupid of me"
she went to him once and said,
        "Do you know that people are raping their children?"
and he said
as he walked out the back door
        "Would you like some tangerines? How about a few zucchinis?"

IT IS TIME FOR NAMING
there are hands
and tongues
and a weight that pressed the life out of her

but then
the weight of a
father upon his five year old daughter
is very
heavy

                                            alyssum

MEMORIES AND SECRETS
Letters between a mother and daughter

My dear daughter,

All your life I treated you and your sister as individuals, always trying to impress upon you to develop your separate talents, to never cease enlarging your minds. Both of you have extremely twisted and incorrect memories of your childhood. No mother was ever prouder of her children. All those years when I worked like four people, I never ceased to have pride in myself and my two wonderful children. I was so proud of my two little girls. It did not matter to me what the sex. They were my own. If you remember, I have said, "I will fight to the death for my own."

Your father started working after school at 14 — he gave what he earned to his widowed mother. He came to Washington at 18, as a messenger boy, went to school nights to earn a degree in accounting — still sending money to his mother. After he died at 38, when I was disposing of his things, I was appalled at the waste of his young life — he had worked so hard and wanted so desperately to get ahead. Yes, he had pride in himself.

Be proud that you are descended from some of the most handsome and most progressive nationalities on earth — pure Celt (Scottish); the great, talented, realistic French (and as you know, Oh Lord, how proud they are of themselves — also smart — they want to keep France French); and English-Welsh. Be proud of that heritage. Is this being racist? I am a reader of history.

I know what is happening to America and the white race all over the world, but particularly here. Before your life is over you will see what I mean. The white race is committing suicide. White women are refusing to have their own children. The people with the best minds are refusing to have their own children. You'd better think about these things I have said, now and previous to this time.

As one grows older all one has to look forward to is a future in one's grandchildren. Yes, I produced, and you could produce "prime specimens." If your father had been older than I and had been able to acquire some financial security before marriage, I would definitely have had at least one other child, regardless of its sex. I wanted my children so much.

You cannot imagine what it is like to have children for a man who does not want them. Although I never regretted your birth, I wanted a boy. The generations cannot be cast aside. I have been punished terribly because I did not honor and go to my mother — even though she was terribly cruel and jealous of me when I was growing up. I remember when my girls were only 18, before my world crashed about my head — my darling girls. No woman ever loved her children more than I, but there is a limit to what one will accept even from one's own children. This is the last letter I shall write you, unless I hear from you. I have been bruised over the last ten years. I cannot take much more.

I received the pretty shell box. I hope you made it. Part of my grief about you, except I wish you were close, is that I believe you are neglecting all of your artistic talents. About "liking" what you are, I always thought you a wonderful, brilliant child; but as a mother I cannot help worrying about your future.

If you ever get pregnant, please do not destroy your child. I would even help you raise it. If you destroy it, when you are old you will bitterly regret it. A child should be greeted with joy. I always stood by you and wanted you to have advantages that I had not had, although my parents did the same for me. I really loved being with you and wanted more time with you than I had. I am sorry you had to be latchkey kids.

You'd better think about the things I have said, now and previous to this time. I am nearly 72 years old, a diabetic who must take care of myself to prevent complications, and my eyesight is failing. I am developing a cataract on one eye. I wonder, after all these years, forgetting the above sentence, what one woman is supposed to put up with. I faced the things that happened to me, accepting my life and whatever responsibilities that entailed, and went on. One has to accept life; no life is perfect. My God, I was an innocent. I really thought I gave you a happy childhood, and, above all, I trusted you and your sister implicitly. I have found out, here and there, that trust was mislaid.

Yes, I am nearly 72 years old, and even if late, have been trying to make a life for myself which is more *me*. At last I have had time to make a few friends, which I never had time for while you were growing up. I know now I was wrong to give of myself to that extent — but I never thought it would cause you and your sister to dislike me so much. I never intended to hang on to you in any way. If you remember correctly (the evidence indicates that you do not) I tried to help each of you develop your distinctive talents, realizing that you were such different individuals. I am appalled at how you have destroyed yourself—don't blame it on your childhood. Your father died, yes, and it was a devastating experience when you were 7. Do you not know it was for me too, especially that I had to leave my children and go to work? But, how I tried, and gave of myself to make up for that fact. Whether you and your sister have any respect for those years, I respect myself for them. I wonder how many present-day women will respect themselves when they are 72 years old. But, then, women today no longer believe in that kind of commitment.

You have always been practically a genius, my dear. I have always known you could be a fine artist or almost anything you put your mind to. Whatever problems you have developed after you left home — obviously to put as many miles between you and me as possible — you did to yourself. For 15 years I have been fighting depression because of my daughter's lack of love for me, and worrying over you and what you were doing to yourself. If what I am is what has disturbed you, then that is just too bad. I was never anything but good to you. It would seem that you might at least let me have a little peace in my last good years.

Your main problem, possibly, is you realize you have wasted your beautiful youth. Well, nothing can be done about that, but you can accept the fact and stop blaming your childhood for it. The years are inexorable. How well I know. And your father, who had the whole burden of his mother and younger brothers put on his shoulders at 14 years of age, never stopped loving her and his family.

I have made many mistakes concerning my life, I know, but one goes on, and I do not blame others for my mistakes in judgment. But my main drive in life was to see that you missed nothing because of your father's death and to give you advantages I did not have. You are extremely beautiful, extremely intelligent and talented. I was happy when I learned you were studying art because I always knew you were artistic, and that you had stopped smoking and were jogging — I hope you have not stopped these activities.

I remember so many sweet things about you and shall always love the lovely girl you have been. You did not have a bad childhood. I did my very best for you. When, if ever, you are able to communicate with me as a daughter should, I am ready and willing to hear from you. You'd better think about the things I have said, now and previous to this time.

As ever, with love,
Mother

Mother,

Your words twisted my childhood memories into terrible secrets, secrets even unto myself. Your words always told me you knew me better than I knew myself — and I believed you. Your words turned my child-molester father into an angel called early to heaven. Your words glorified our ancient past for the wrong reasons. Your words taught me to hate others in order to feel superior. Your words taught me to hate myself.

Your words endlessly threatened me. Your words created a world of isolation which separated us from the rest of the world. Your words told me life was imperfect without a man — no matter how imperfect the man. Your words belied the reality that you did not want me, and your act of attempted infanticide. Your words intimated I was the cause of your suffering and I would be punished.

Your words tried to erase my memories of traumatic events. Your words never gave without taking away. Your words convinced me to abort to keep another from experiencing what I had. I did not then know I could break the chain. Your words substituted love for other things.

Your words clouded your vision — created a world you could accept. Your words turned the slightest mischief into a capital crime. Your words accused me of your own transgressions against yourself. Your words enforced a remembering that was correct only to you. Your words of incessant encouragement buried my creativity along with my true feelings. One cannot exist without the other.

Your words attempted to eradicate your guilt and complicity. Your words would not accept whatever respect and gratitude I did have for you. Your words were ludicrous when speaking of trust and commitment. Your words made me afraid of trying any endeavor for fear I would not live up to your expectations. Your words projected on me your own inadequacies.

Your words were sometimes wise out of context. Your words contradicted themselves. Your words claimed ownership of my victories. Your words convoluted, perverted, entangled, maimed, and buried me. Your words were never a two-way communication device.

Renee

INSIGHTS AND PERCEPTIONS

Silent screams can now be heard. In speaking out, we begin to heal ourselves and help others to understand the trauma of sexual abuse. Your inner self holds the depth of your experiences; focus on what is coming from inside and allow it to be projected from you. The sound can range from whispers to roars — whatever the volume, the magnitude is great. Telling is therapeutically healing, for when you state your own truths you validate your inner self.

It is important to listen to how you feel and give voice to what is heard. Speaking out comes with risks, but the rewards can be profound.

Finding words to communicate who you are can be compared to using a muscle that has been immobilized for a long period. It needs to be worked gradually and gently at first before getting back to normal use. So it is with speaking out. At first be cautious with whom you choose to share. Make sure they value you and your process. As you gain strength the need for caution will not be so important. You will be grounded in your own reality. You hold the truth.

BE REAL

C H A P T E R   T W E L V E

NURTURING YOURSELF

"To love myself for all that I am, for all that I might be."

Karen S. Cronk

LIFE

Once I was a vase . . .
Whole . . . intact . . .
Waiting to be filled
With the spring of life.
Then I was shattered
And all that I contained
Flowed out
And was lost.
Now with gentleness
and skill . . .
You are gathering the pieces
Placing them together . . .
Binding them with love . . .
Filling me with light.

Once I was only a vase.

Anonymous

To Love Myself

WHY was it so hard?
So hard to wrap my arms around myself
To love myself for all that I am,
For all that I might be.

WHY was it so hard?
To accept the hurt and crying child,
To let her know it was all right
To feel and to be.

WHY was it so hard?
So hard to feel that she was a welcome and wondrous
Part, to treasure her wide-eyed innocence,
And unwavering trust of the heart.

WHY was it so hard?
So hard to realize that she alone could view the world,
As fresh and new each day,
To appreciate her gloriously
Curious way.

WHY was it so hard?
So hard to truly love myself,
For all that I am,
For all that I might be.
So hard to believe,
That she, after all,
            Is ME.

Karen S. Cronk

SURVIVORS' GROUP

What does it mean to be an adult survivor of child abuse? It means looking in the mirror and seeing garbage, if you see anything at all. It means finding ways to numb yourself so you don't have to feel or think. It means being afraid to go to sleep in the dark, or without a weapon at hand. It means waking night after night because of nightmares or because you sense evil in your room. It means thinking that you are crazy because sane people sleep in the dark and are not afraid of things that go bump in the night. It means keeping yourself so busy that your head is full of static white noise that drowns out the screaming child that lives inside you.

We sat that first Monday evening in a large, softly-lit room, some dozen women who had come together uneasily, if not reluctantly, to speak of our dirty little secrets. In the following weeks our tales were told in bits and pieces. They were terrifying stories of abuse by fathers, grandfathers, mothers, uncles, cousins, brothers, friends, neighbors. We cried and shook. Our backs and bellies hurt. We felt we might suffocate. We clenched our teeth. We were cold, hot, raw, vulnerable, angry, sad, and afraid. We comforted and confronted each other with hugs, laughter, honesty and the recognition of shared experiences. We felt safe.

We found that we had dealt with our particular pain in ways that numbed us and still allowed us to go on more or less well. Some of us forgot, repressed what had happened to us and are only now remembering. That makes us feel crazy but we are not. Some of us have misused drugs and alcohol. That makes us feel weak but we are not. We have continued to abuse our own bodies and spirits years after the other horror has stopped. That makes us feel bad but we are not.

So we came together to think about ourselves; to try to find the person inside each of us who is truly our own, that self free of our defensiveness that enables us to survive. We came together and said to each other, "You are not alone. You are not crazy, you are not vile, dirty or defective. You had no control over what happened to you, it was not your fault." And we said, "You are good. You are clean and bright. You are lovable. You are loved." We learned to believe it.

Suzanne Chamberlin McKnight

BROKEN PIECES

I sleep with my kitty — little Mau. She is my child, my friend, my littlest love. She meets me at the gate whenever I come home and rolls on her back so I can rub her tummy. I think that Mau loves me too — and that's so special. When I take a nap on the sofa, she curls up on my chest to sleep. She gets pissed off if I move, glares for a moment, closes her eyes and falls back to sleep. Sometimes I wake up at night in a panic — Mau is sleeping between my legs and I feel crowded, tense, invaded. I move her quickly and close up my legs. I feel bad — she thinks it's comfortable there and I make her move. She loves me, I think; but that doesn't mean I have to let her be close to me everywhere. With Mau, I can say no.

I have been sick this week, stayed home from work. It's been a relief, not facing the hatred, the silence, the wall of isolation. I do good work (I know I do — I don't give myself compliments easily). I took this job in a wild grasp for stability. Steady paycheck. Consistent work. A job I could leave at the end of the day, to have time to think, to identify feelings. But then the wall was built and I felt trapped. I am scared of this feeling that I've had before; and I wonder if all the feelings come back to the old one. Maybe nothing changes, it just gets bigger. I feel sad. So I'm home from work, hiding in my home with Mau, feeling safe, feeling trapped, reaching out every few hours to assure myself that I'm not alone.

I went to the doctor this week because it was so hard to breathe. I asked a friend to take me, because I was in pain, because I was scared. The doctor had to put his hands on me before passing judgment. "You are sick, I can hear how hard it is for you to breathe." Relief. He believed me — I'm really sick. I am not faking, I am not crazy, it was okay to see a doctor this time. It's okay to feel pain, this time — it's real.

It was very different, the last time I saw my therapist. I spoke of things I never mentioned before. I made connections I was always afraid of. I talked about suicide in a new way, wanting to be listened to, so the deciding times didn't hurt so much. I talked about different pain — my uncle, my brother, the doctors, my mother, my friends. I talked of feeling crazy and different, and all alone. I told her of the time I learned that people liked themselves, and what a shock it was. I hurt so bad — it was something everyone knew but me.

I wanted to cry as all these memories tumbled out. But I don't really cry. I wanted her to hold me, but I didn't want to ask, I was afraid she might. I might cry if she did. I made up jokes to ease the pain and the flow of pictures rushing into my head. All my memories were connected to different houses and states, that was how I remembered. I wanted that to be funny, so it would hurt less. She told me what I went through was bad, and it was understandable that I was so tired. I think it's the first time I ever heard that. The pain was real; I am not crazy, not faking it — it's real pain. I left feeling very different, like something important happened. I wanted to call her and tell her but I didn't.

Mommy, I don't want to feel bad for what they did to me. I don't want to remember hands on little girl's secret places that I didn't understand. I don't want to remember being too little to be touched too hard. I don't want to remember those games and big fights. I don't want to remember threats for fighting back. I don't want to remember being dragged out of the closet to visit relatives I was afraid of. I don't want to remember that you never noticed my silence, my tears. Mommy, I don't want to remember that I told you — and you did nothing. Mommy, you told me no one would ever love me as much as my family. That scares me, Mommy. I don't want to be loved like that.

I wanted to be loved. I want to have fun. I don't want to be a child anymore; I don't want to be their victim, their survivor. I want to grow up. I don't want to fight the need to cut myself. I don't want to force myself to leave the house. I don't want to decide to live or die. I don't want to have to hurt myself because of old anger. I want it all to go away. I'm tired now, I want to sleep without your hands coming down on my body. I want a break. I want you to take it all away from me, Mommy — give it back to them. I want you all to feel bad so I can go out and play.

Deborah Lynn

PROGRESS REPORT ON DEBORAH

Since I first wrote this piece, I've grown up and moved beyond the abuse that controlled much of my life and actions. This last summer, I completed more than ten years of therapy. Alyce and I had a wonderful dinner to celebrate! As I used to believe I was destined to live in a fog forever or to die, that night was very significant for me.

Critical to my recovery was reliving and accepting some of the feelings I experienced as a child. Facing those fears and the depth of my abuse was the most painful thing I have faced as an adult. I learned through this process that healing was my responsibility, even though the abuse was never my fault. I worked like hell for that healing and I feel grateful that there can be so many good days in my life.

I now manage a farm with my partner and am also Direct Services Coordinator for a rape crisis center in Southern California. It has been a longtime goal of mine to be strong enough and capable enough to give something back to the community that supported me so well during my healing and growing.

We were barely there...
pale, faceless,
with no words...

Sandra Joel Ahrens

SOMETIMES THE KNIGHT

(This poem is for those who go through our pain with us)

Sometimes the knight
grows weary
With fending off the night
and the terror of it.
Grows tired of
the inexhaustible distress
of damsels who are needy
without wanting, who are passionate without desire.
Whose stark eyes tell more
than one wants to bear,
Whose prisons are themselves
whose dragons are elusive
and never finally slain.
Sometimes the knight
must defend his own honor
Against those who find him
and name him champion
And then
can't believe him.
Sometimes the knight
cries "Enough!"
at the bottomless need
of his dark ladies;

at their spiraling descent

at their retreats at night.

And in the afternoon

instead of being

For God's sake just there,

and okay for once

Sometimes the knight

doubts his calling

When the damsel's desire to die

so real and so imagined

Invades him.

He knows how little bandages he's got

And that he must prop

the frail crutch

of belief in the knight

Up under the chasm

that seeks not to know herself.

Sometimes the knight

must rescue himself

And rest from the quest of the grail.

He feeds himself steak and stiff bourbon,

Watching the game

he waits

for the next call to rescue.

Sandra Joel Ahrens

WAR BUDDIES

I'd been ironing that night
trying to put creases
in his shirts
just in case . . .
he decided to go
look for a job.

I felt so tired
finally sat down
and gently touched my stomach
in which you rested
speaking softly to you
I did that a lot
Telling you how much
I loved you already
Anticipating the feel of you
in my arms
Oh how they ached to hold you!

He came home
Loaded again
Armed with
his pistoled fists
Ready to fire
Both guns
At the drop of a hat
or
an innocent spoken word

He said
I'd whored around!
Told me to
Get an abortion
He yelled,
"That ain't my kid!"

Afterwards
after he had unleashed
his pent-up anger
on me/us
I laid down on the double bed
Trying to find sleep
Trying to give me/us
peace
Rocking us slowly
Crooning, "I love you"
Calling you,
"My baby,"
Telling you,
"Don't worry, we'll be all right,"
"Me and you, we'll make it,"

Then
as the words were spoken
I felt
a tiny quiver
your first movement
Your answering to my
thoughts and feelings

At that moment
I knew
We'd always have
a special bond
that no man
could ever break
We'd be all right
Somehow . . .

And then you were two
And afterwards
again
After he grew tired
of hitting me
again
I laid down on the double bed
you next to me
You laid your head on my breast
You patted my stomach
your once-upon-a-time home
And you told me
in your wise little man voice,
"We'll make it Mama,"
"Me 'n' you,"
"We'll be all right."

Donna McGrew
Dedicated to my son Daniel
for giving me strength
when I needed it most.

INSIGHTS AND PERCEPTIONS

It is hard to accept that you have needs when all your life they have not been met and your focus has been on meeting the needs of others. You cannot recapture what you did not get, no matter how hard you try or whom you look to. You can never go back and be that child again. A deep sense of loss and sadness accompanies that realization. Feel the tears.

But with this realization also comes an opportunity to find the nurturing parent inside you. Now is the time to learn a new skill that was meant as a gift to you when you were born. Instead of relying on others to provide comfort, look inside to get your needs met. You must be your own best friend. In truth, you know yourself and what you need better than anyone else. Care for yourself. Listen to yourself. Accept yourself. Take yourself out. Rock yourself. Hug yourself.

This does not mean doing it alone. We are on this earth together. Strength comes from relying on and also helping others. It is perfectly fine at times to be dependent, needy, and weak. Having a therapist to support, guide and teach you is very helpful as you are learning about nurturing. Allow yourself to be taken care of in that therapeutic relationship, and do not fall back into taking care of your therapist.

There are people around you who can help you, hold you, and sometimes carry you. Let that happen. Most importantly, care for your hurt and crying child.

BE LOVING

CHAPTER THIRTEEN

BEYOND THE DARKNESS

"Recognizing that we were not to blame means accepting the fact that those whom we loved did not have our best interest at heart."

Ellen Bass
Laura Davis

MEMORIAL DAY

I am discovering my holidays one by one and I am making preparations for the ones which roll over me relentlessly year by year, without regard for my feelings or my life circumstances.

I say, "I lived through another Mother's Day." I regard it as a miracle. I fired my mother more than two years ago as part of my recovery process from my incest experience. She has bonded with the perpetrators.

And then there is my mothering which is also lost. I gave up my daughter because I wasn't a good enough mother to understand that I was not fit to parent her. I knew this even though I had not yet understood that the incest in my life and family made this true. Now she belongs to another woman who raised her and who has earned the right to my daughter's Mother's Day celebration.

My middle sister sent me a Mother's Day card and I was touched, humbled and a little guilty that I had not done the same for her. My younger sister and

I had agreed that we were still in a state of rebellion against the holiday card tradition since our mother had been merciless in her celebration of each minute occasion on the calendar. We were enraged by her paper mothering, she did not even write her own words to us, but she does not send us these profanities any more. "Next year," I tell myself, "I won't be so reactionary and I'll be ready to send Margaret a Mother's Day card." I do respect her mothering.

This is the first Memorial Day I have ever properly celebrated, if that's the word. I went to three graves and I threw flowers into a creek bed and I built two stone cairns in a lemon grove and I went on a picnic and I listened to a flute trembling and warbling sweet music. I was silent and quiet, and I remembered the three young women who were murdered and their bodies dumped alongside the mountain roads nine years before. I was the director of a women's center at that time.

"We remember you, Regina," my friend and I whispered as we threw mustard blossoms and Queen Anne's Lace into the creek bed below us. "We remember you, Rita and Janie," we said as we built the stones into a pile and surrounded them with fresh lemons and sprigs from the trees. The lemon scent was pungent and festive under the warm May sun, and my little dog pressed himself next to my heart as he sat in my lap. He did this to remind me I was alive, and I thanked him.

As we drove away I knew that my dream of the Tomb of the Unknown Woman had been realized at last and that I had finally created a Memorial Day with meaning for me.

Father's Day lies in wait, like the beast my father was. The telephone company has a new telephone commercial which tells a tender story of a father and a daughter, and the woman's voice saying, "Daddy, Daddy!" in dulcet tones. I experience intense longing and sadness, which I recognize as the same feeling of loss I experienced upon finding my daughter shortly after her eighteenth birthday. (I waited until then to seek her out.)

The finding of my daughter was also the losing of her. Eighteen years which could never be reclaimed or replaced or experienced. The finding of my incest experience was also the losing of my illusions of family and fatherhood, with the attendant grief and pain.

This is not to say that I dwell upon my losses or my grief but that now I honor the truth of my life; I am free to experience happiness. The denial of my grief had meant a denial of all of my other feelings, and that meant the living dead, which is the overriding characteristic of the inner life of both of my parents.

I honor the father and mother within myself and I do not accept the status of orphan/victim.

Next comes my birthday, which has always been a good day for me. I had an easy birth, announcing myself in a cherry tree where my mother had clambered to pick cherries. I did not arrive in the tree itself but quickly, a few hours later, in the hospital. My June birthday is awash in images of sunlight and lilac bushes, apple trees and farms, ocean views and long, long summer days with faint evening stars. I have decided to ask my daughter if we can make my birthday and hers a holiday. I must do this lightly because she is still a teenager. Still "cool." Still struggling for identity.

I asked her to come and visit me on her birthday in November and she said, "But how did you know that it was my birthday?"

Then we both laughed. "One thing I do know about you is your birthday." We are, after all, strangers.

She came with her boyfriend whom she uses as a buffer between us, and I gave her a T-shirt with a painting on it and she went away happily. I court her slowly, delicately. Her adopted mother is jealous and fearful and I do not wish to divide my daughter between us.

I have nothing to say about the fourth of July or Labor Day. My red-haired sister's birthday falls in August and I enjoy that. I am safe until Thanksgiving Day which tosses me over to Christmas and then I am thrown into group holidays and my entire relationship to family is confronted once more.

Last year I recognized, for the first time, that I had passed over into my victim state and that there was another state of mind I had achieved which was not-victim. I could experience the victim state. "I'm in the Twilight Zone," I announced. It lasted ten days altogether and came on right after Thanksgiving and right before Christmas.

Since I understood that I had passed over, I was able to tend to myself and not thrash about wildly, as I had every other year, injuring myself on the rocks of past hurts and my own indecisions about what to do with myself. Before incest therapy I just hurt myself without knowing why or what or even that I was in my victim state. I hurt myself by drinking, by eating, by smoking dope, by denying my feelings, by visiting my mother who required my violence and compliance in life, by getting sick, by depression, by remembering my father weaving in front of the Christmas tree drunk, by feeling sorry for myself, by knowing that I was defective because I hadn't married and so I had no family of my own.

But this season I tended myself. I stayed home in my new house. My first house, not rented, but owned by me. "I am my family," I said. My friend came over with her son and she covered her hurt about Christmas and Christmas trees by pretending to be Jewish and therefore indifferent. But I knew better and her nine-year-old son gave us both ample opportunities to buy a tree and decorate it and play games and roast a turkey and go to the beach and call up everybody we liked. I dressed up in a red hat and red dress with a black belt and black boots and took my white poodle to the photographers and sat for a portrait which was my Christmas card. "Happy Holidays from Annie and Fuzzy."

I called my redhead sister and wept and begged, "Mother me, mother me." She did. My younger sister and I compared our struggles in the Twilight Zone and laughed with that strange redeeming humor that only the incest survivor understands. My middle sister blessed me in her courteous way and I allowed myself the gray and numbing grief of the losing of the other six: my mother, my father, my littlest sister, my three brothers.

The New Year came and I was safe. "I lived through the Holidays!" This was a surprise to me. Now only my mother's birthday lies ahead but that is only a pinch since I no longer take responsibility for her life and, besides, her birthday lies next to Darlene's and I focus on that joyfully because she is a true sister and a fellow traveler.

Then there is Groundhog Day and Easter which I like because I am always enamored by the notion of resurrection and rebirth no matter what my decisions about organized religion may be. So it goes until I am faced with Mother's Day once again.

Perhaps my discovery of Memorial Day, which fits neatly between Mother's Day and Father's Day, will assuage my grief slowly and softly year by year. For I too am a force, and I too am able to wear down rock with the gentle pressure of my remembrance.

Patricia Ann Murphy

PROGRESS REPORT ON PATRICIA

I am recovered! I use group therapy and body work including massage, rebirthing, and yoga in my process. I also use journal work.

My first novel is the story of a family in its recovery from childhood sexual abuse. *Searching for Spring* was published by The Naiad Press in September, 1987. My second novel will also be published by The Naiad Press in September of 1988. *We Walk the Back of the Tiger* is a story of a serial murderer and his impact on a community of women.

I continue in private practice as a vocational rehabilitation counselor in the California Workers' Compensation system.

I live quietly and happily with my poodle and my computer in Southern California.

BUDS OF FORGIVENESS

Grandpa touched me and left me
>   wanting more.
Years of yearning —
>   Spending pearls —
>   for the same empty desire.
Repeating . . .
Now face-to-face it is known,
>   Embraced with so many years of searching and denial
>   for what would not be understood, until
In this moment, it is set free.

New leaves, tender buds
>   Spring of newness and awakening all that is lovely and
Blooming without the flaw
>   from the summer the twisted blight touched
>   a small and perfect tree.

Mary

EXCERPTS FROM A CEREMONY

For the ending of a relationship between a daughter and her mother

On my forty-first birthday I wrote my mother: "The lack of truth in our relationship really bothers me because it feels like we are pretending we have a good, close relationship. We do this because we both want it to be so. But this is unreal. I know you feel very bad about that, as do I. I want us either to work at being honest and telling each other our truth and hearing the other's truth, or else be completely separate. I sense we need to cry together to get over our many past hurts and misunderstandings. Then I hope we could finally trust enough for our bodies to relax into softness when we hug. That is what I really want most."

Mother replied, "We're not pretending we have a 'close relationship' — perhaps you are. We have accepted that our ways are not for you and that you want to go a different way. So be it — get on with your life. Be the free spirit you want to be. You must live your life as you see fit — but remember that we, too, should have the same right."

Our relationship is dead. I have a mother no longer. Free at last, free at last, great God almighty, free at last.

I'd never forgotten the beatings that I received monthly when I was five to twelve, with a razor strap (most often), belts, books, hair brushes, kitchen utensils, and once a shingle. I knew I had to remember so I wouldn't repeat them with my own children. Mother had always said of course I would hit my children. "If you don't they turn out bad."

For over three years now I've been painfully recovering a completely new set of memories, of incest with my father, lasting some eight years. If it were not for hearing other women tell the truth about their lives, I wouldn't have found the courage to believe my own perceptions, the messages coming to me from the senses of my body, from whom I've long been disconnected, the memories my body's been giving back to me.

I must begin to put together these two different pictures of my past, of incest with my father and repeated beatings by my mother. I believe these two separate pictures I have of my childhood are indeed "the severed parts" of one whole: my own past.

Daddy felt Mother gave too much attention to us, and so he didn't feel properly loved or cared for as a husband should always be. And he saw that my sister and I loved him whole-heartedly, especially when Mother seemed completely occupied with her new boy baby.

Daddy is a much more physically close person than Mother, and I particularly liked this. As he more and more openly preferred my company to Mother's, she was hurt and became angry and cold with me. His preferring me also gave me the strength to defy Mother a lot. I often felt more powerful than she, and I knew she couldn't make me do anything I really didn't want to. I even said this to her sometimes. So the start of the incest with Daddy caused the deterioration of my relationship with Mother.

This was very early, around age three.

I must tell the truth about how things were between us as best I know it. It must be good enough. I must be good enough. I have recovered one memory that helps "to put the severed parts together."

I remember when Daddy came home unexpectedly in the middle of the night, and I was sleeping in bed with you, Mother. I loved that. It always felt wonderful, lying warm and close to you all night. You immediately wanted to take me out, but he was angry and wouldn't let you. Did you already know what would happen? You two had an argument, and he ended up raping you right beside me in the bed. You fought and protested throughout about my being there, without success. When he discovered I was awake he wanted to molest me. He hit you to shut you up. I remember you crying next to him while he did those things to me. Then you said, "Stop it, you're hurting her." You were right, but when he hurt me more and said, "I'm not hurting you, am I?" I felt forced to lie and agree with him that it didn't hurt. Then he stopped, and you carried me to my own bed, where you stayed awhile holding me. As you left you said, "He doesn't mean to do these things; he can't help himself. He's really a good man."

The truth is this good man had just raped you, his wife, while I watched, and then molested me, his daughter, while you watched. I call what he did to you torture and what he did to me being tortured. And it is true that this rapist and child molester who is my father and your husband, and with whom you still live, is in many ways a good man. But he is at the same time a sadistic torturer who rapes and abuses women and girls, even those he says he loves.

You taught me, Mother, to comply with the patriarchy of self-hatred, and lack of love and respect for other women. Now I burn up these false gifts I received too young. This frees me to acknowledge and celebrate the good things I received from you and other women who have nurtured me. I believe in my own ability to love now. That's the most important gift I carry with me.

Mother, I want to remember you as you really were, all you gave to me, both the gifts I'll always value and those I now refuse. I remember both your love and caring for me, but you felt you also had to fulfill your duties as a wife to that good man, your husband.

We are all children of one mother, daughters of the earth who always supports us. I belong here on this planet, in this world. What I feel is real, what I remember really happened, all the parts of it. I am not crazy, though I see things other people don't and sometimes I even say them out loud. I can recover my body, reconnect with my feelings. I am real, and I am good.

Pegasis

PROGRESS REPORT ON PEGASIS

I currently live in Oregon with my teenaged daughter. I am working with disabled senior citizens, helping them to stay out of nursing homes. I have been unable to continue doing the therapy I feel I need, because of a lack of money. I am happy with my life.

Editor's note: *"Knowing It Wasn't Our Fault"* and *"The Little Girl Within"* are sections from the book *"The Courage to Heal: A Guide for Women Survivors of Child Sexual Abuse"* published by Harper and Row in 1988.

Ellen Bass is co-editor of "I Never Told Anyone: Writings by Woman Survivors of Child Sexual Abuse," and facilitates workshops for survivors nationwide. Laura Davis is a writer and radio producer who is also a survivor working on her own healing.

Although they have collaborated on the writing of both these chapters, the first is written from Ellen's perspective as a counselor, and the second is written from Laura's as a survivor.

KNOWING IT WASN'T OUR FAULT

Children often believe they are to blame for being sexually abused. As adult survivors, many of us continue to hold that belief. Although large numbers of children are abused, it is never the fault of any one of them. Yet there are many reasons why we assume that blame.

Some of us were told explicitly that it was our fault. We were told we were bad, nasty, dirty. That's why we were being abused. We were told we were doing something wrong, and that it was bad, so no one could know. It would kill Mommy. Daddy would be sent away. We were told we fantasized it because we wanted it. We were punished when someone did find out. If we ever said anything, we were told we made up horrible lies. Or the subject was never discussed, giving us the message that it was too terrible to talk about.

For some of us, the religions in which we were raised told us we were sinners, unclean, damned to hell. We became convinced we were evil, ruined, unlovable even to God.

"That little incested girl inside of me is still waiting for the lightning to strike because I told people what happened to me. If I say 'I think it was my dad,' I'll burn up in hell-fire."

One small child was even begged by her abuser to stop him. He kept telling her how wrong it was and that she must not let him do it ever again — and then he'd force her once more.

There are also less obvious reasons why we blame ourselves. It is a stark and terrifying realization for a child to see how vulnerable and powerless she actually is. Thinking that we were bad, that we had some influence on how we were treated, gave us a sense of control, though illusory, and perceiving ourselves as bad allowed us the future possibility that we could become good, and thus things could improve. In truth, nothing we did caused the abuse. Nothing within our power could ever have stopped the abuse. Our world was an unsafe place where adults were untrustworthy and out of control, where our well-being and sometimes our very lives were in danger.

This perspective, though realistic, is more distressing for many children than just thinking the adults in our lives did something wrong. For if there is no hope that the people in our lives whose job it is to love and protect us will do so, where can we turn?

"To feel in second grade that the people you would come to for comfort, or to ask a question, are the same people who are willing to hurt you, and torture you, and possibly kill you is too overwhelming. I felt I was really evil. It's almost like those child devil movies, like *Damian.* Inside this innocent little girl is this evil seed. I used to think that just my presence made people feel bad and made bad things happen. I used to think that if only I did something then everything would change. If only I got straight A's then my dad would stop hurting me. I felt I could control things by my behavior. No one around me seemed to be controlling anything. I still have this really warped sense of what I can do with my presence or my actions."

Recognizing that we were not to blame means accepting the fact that those whom we loved did not have our best interest at heart. So painful was it for us to give up that love that we often chose to shoulder the guilt ourselves.

The extremities to which we have gone to construct explanations of why it's really our fault are sometimes shocking. One woman told me, "I know I was only five years old, but I was an extremely intelligent five-year-old. I should have been able to figure out a way to escape." To anyone else this sounds absurd, but this woman was still holding the firm belief that she was at fault. And she was still ashamed.

Another woman blamed herself because at the age of 12 she said "No," and her father stopped. "Why couldn't I have done that right away, at four, when he started?" she chastised herself. "I did have the power to stop him."

Another woman answered her, "I said 'no' and my father never stopped. I fought and kicked and screamed 'no.' But abusers don't stop because you say 'no.' They stop when they're ready to stop. By the time you were 12 your father was ready to stop. Maybe he only liked small children. You had less control than you think."

Women blame themselves because they took money, gifts, or special privileges. But if we were able to get some small thing back I think we should, instead, give ourselves credit. One woman in a workshop was given a bicycle by her abuser. On it she was able to ride away from her house, out to the woods, and there feel the safety of the trees. She blamed herself for having taken the bicycle. I commend her for taking what she could get in that wasteland.

Many of us hold particularly shameful feelings if we needed attention and affection and did not fight off sexual advances because of those needs. Or if we sought out the affection. The closeness may have felt good to us. We may have adored our abusers. We may have loved feeling like Mommy's special girl. I hear women say, "I'm the one who asked for a back rub," or "I kept going back," or "I climbed into bed with him."

But we were not wrong. Every child needs attention. Every child needs affection. If these are not offered in healthy, nonsexual ways, children will take them in whatever ways they can find them because they are essential needs.

There was a scientific experiment conducted in which infants were fed and diapered, but not held. The experiment had to be interrupted because the infants were losing weight so quickly that they were in danger of dying. The need for touch, for contact, is so great that babies clearly cannot live without it.

Although some of us felt only pain or numbness when we were abused, many of us experienced sensual or sexual pleasure, arousal, and orgasm. Even though the experience may have been confusing, frightening, or devastating, we may also have felt some degree of pleasurable feelings. For many, this aspect of the abuse has been one of the most difficult to share.

One woman told me she skimmed *I Never Told Anyone* cover to cover to see if anyone else had had an orgasm while being abused. She urgently needed to know that she wasn't the only one. Since then hundreds of women have talked to me about these feelings and most of them have been ashamed.

What's important for us to recognize is that it is natural to have had sexual feelings, and that even if we had had sexual responses to the abuse and even if those responses felt good, it still doesn't mean that we are in any way responsible. Our bodies are created to respond to stimulation. When we are touched sexually, our physiology — nerves, synapses, muscles, blood — is designed to give us pleasure. These are natural bodily responses over which we do not always have control. When we eat a sandwich, our stomachs digest the sandwich. We can't stop our stomachs from digesting the sandwich. In a similar way, when we're stimulated sexually, we can't always stop our bodies from responding.

One woman was raped at knife-point and experienced orgasm. This is not a statement that she wanted to be raped or liked it. This is not a statement that sexual pleasure is bad. And, very importantly, it is not a betrayal of her body. Her body did what bodies are supposed to do. We were betrayed not by our bodies, but by the adults who abused us.

It is unfair to expect children to be able to protect themselves. Children do a lot of testing. They test limits. They test our attitudes. This is their job. They develop a sense of what the world is all about through this testing. And it is *always* the responsibility of the adults to behave with respect towards children.

If a sixteen-year-old girl walks into her living room naked and throws herself on her father, he is still not justified in touching her sexually. A responsible father would say, "There seems to be a problem here," would tell the girl to get clothes on and discuss it with her, getting professional help if necessary. Regardless of age or circumstance, there is never an excuse for sexually abusing a child. It is still totally and absolutely the responsibility of the adult not to be sexual with the children.

As children we did not have the skills or power to protect ourselves. Today, at least there are child assault prevention programs in school which teach children to be safe, strong, and free. Now many parents are teaching their children that they have the right to say "No." But it is only recently that children have been provided with even these few basic tools. No woman I have worked with has been told, as a child, that she had the right to control her body. Even those of us who did resist or try to fight back often encountered increased coercion. Yet we still blame ourselves.

The next time you're in a schoolyard, look around for children the age you were when the abuse began. Watch the way they interact. Listen to the pitch of their voices. Look at their actual size. Do you honestly think one of those children deserves to be abused?

As adults still believing the abuse was our fault, we have lost touch with the simplicity of a child's longing to share love. When my daughter was about six, we were riding in the car on the way to visit friends and she told me she wanted to be my lover. I knew her concept of lover was somewhat fuzzy, but she had enough idea to feel she wanted that. I responded gently that it wasn't possible. She quickly added, "I know I'm too small, but when I'm grown up."

"No," I explained. "Even when you grow up, I'll still be your mom and you'll still be my daughter. We have a special relationship that will never change. We can never be lovers, but we will always love each other in our own special way."

"Yes," she assented, "that will never change." Then, as she got out of the car she turned to me. "Mom, don't say anything to them about what we talked about. Okay?"

I took her hand as we walked to the house. "Of course not."

This is the innocent love that abusers exploit.

◆ ◆ ◆ ◆

THE LITTLE GIRL WITHIN

When I heard people talk about forgiving the child within, I raised my left eyebrow and thought, "California." There was no little girl inside of me. And if there were one, she was too weak and helpless for me to want to know her. She'd been the one who'd gotten me into this. She was a troublemaker and I wanted nothing to do with her.

Many survivors have a very difficult time with the concept of the child within, though forgiving that child is an essential part of the healing. Too often we blame her, hate her, or ignore that she exists at all. We hate ourselves for having been small, for having needed affection, for having let ourselves be abused.

For many of us, even acknowledging the fact that we were once children can be very threatening. It means remembering a time when we did not have the power to protect ourselves. It means remembering our shame, our vulnerability and our pain. It means acknowledging that the abuse really happened.

"For a long time, I hadn't been able to realize that I had ever been a child at all. My therapist had me bring in photographs of my childhood. She'd say, 'See. This is you. This is something that happened to you. Do you see that this child is only this tall? Can you see that this child is you?' Finally, I started to realize that maybe all of this had something to do with me. And that it had happened to me when I was a child, not as an adult."

Another survivor, who'd made her way in the world by being strong and tough, described the process this way:

"It's been painful, because at first the way I would relate to the little girl was by drawing little pictures. Since I could always deal with other people's problems better than my own, she always came out looking really different from me. I'd think about the terrible things that had happened to her, and I'd feel bad for the little girl in the picture, but I would separate that from me.

"But slowly, I'd come to remember what it felt like to have a little body like that, remember what it was like to wear those clothes. I've had to find that softness I lost, or never was able to deal with. I've had to cry those little-girl tears. I've had to get under her skin and that's when the process started getting kind of hard."

My own re-connection to the inner child came through my own interaction with kids. I have always loved children, but for months after I remembered the incest it was too painful to be around them. I'd see them playing, or running down the streets, little girls flipping up their skirts, and showing white cotton panties, and I'd cringe inside. "They're too vulnerable," I'd think. "They're too little."

I remember spending Halloween at my friend's house, just a few months after I had my first memories. I'd fled the trick-or-treaters in my neighborhood. It still hurt too much to see those innocent little faces. They'd say "Trick or Treat," and all I could think was, "Who's going to ruin you?" Every child seems like a target.

The doorbell rang. My friend asked me to get it. It was a mother with a little girl. The girl was dressed as a angel, in a flowing white dress with gold trim. She had straight blonde hair cut in a pageboy. Set on her head was a halo made of aluminum foil and a bent wire hanger. I asked her how old she was. In a tiny little voice, she answered proudly, "Five and a half!"

I couldn't take my eyes off her. She looked exactly like I had when I was her age. It was like looking in a mirror back 25 years. I was transfixed. I just stared at her, until her mother put a protective arm around her shoulder and glared at me. I gave the little girl a Snickers bar and turned away. I shut the door slowly behind them and sat down in the living room, dazed.

All I could think was, "That's how small I was! I was that little when he forced himself on me. I was just a little girl! How could he have done that to me?" I felt tears of outrage and grief. I had been innocent! There was nothing I could have done! I hadn't done anything wrong. None of it had been my fault. "I was only a child," I screamed into the empty living room, as the sudden reality of who a child of five is flooded through me. That little molested girl was me.

Once we recognize that we were molested as children, the next step is making contact with the child who still lives inside us. That wounded little girl bears our name, is locked inside layers of protection. We've made sure no one can get to her anymore. We've safeguarded her.

But not having her in our life means we have lost contact with a part of ourselves. We have not had access to her softness, to her sense of trust and wonder. We have lost her capacity for joy, her spontaneous enjoyment of life. And at the same time, her pain and her confusion have been petrified.

But even more importantly, if we hate her, we're hating ourselves. It is only in learning to take care of her that we learn to take care of ourselves. Until now, she has not felt safe. Until now, no one has listened to her. And though we may start with feelings of mistrust and ambivalence, part of healing is bringing her back into us. A 42-year-old survivor put it this way:

"My child has been silenced for 40 years. I began to hear her crying out in me. She needed someone to listen to her. 'Someone has to listen to me. No one's ever listened to me. No one's ever believed me.' And that was her first need if she was going to heal.

"I began to listen to her and began to honor her and to nurture her and to do nice things for her. She'd been deeply wounded, deeply, deeply wounded. I needed to be her mother. That awakened my own healing energy, and I began to respond to that child: whether she needed to wear soft clothes, to eat an ice cream cone, or watch 'I Love Lucy' or sit out in the flowers. She knew what she needed to heal.

"And this I'm discovering more and more. She will guide me. She knows if she needs to be held. There may be times when she just needs to have her hair brushed. I did as much as I could to take care of her. I held myself. I stroked myself. Or I'd rock. Comfort the child that had been wounded in me. I had to be gentle with myself. My child had been so abused. She didn't need to be whipped to heal."

In Ellen's workshops she suggests that women make contact with the child within through writing. Sometimes the women write a dialogue with the child, first speaking as their adult self to the child they once were, and then allowing the child to answer. Other times they addressed themselves directly to the child within. These writings have been deeply moving. They signal the end to self–blame and self–hatred that has kept so many of us from moving on. Krishnabia wrote the following to her child within:

Dear Little One,

I am so sorry for what you went through. I am so sorry that you had so much pain and isolation. If I had been there, I would have helped you, I would have taken you into my arms and protected you. I would have loved you. But I wasn't there. Please forgive me for not coming until now. I will not let go of your hand again. I take responsibility to take care of you, to shelter you, to protect you. I will meet your needs to the best of my ability. I will honor your sensitivity. You will never be crazy again. Of this, I am certain. You are a strong, courageous spirit and I am honored to be with you.

FIRST WE CREATE THE NIGHTMARES, THEN WE CREATE THE PRISONS

That afternoon as Susan began to read aloud, she cried after almost every sentence. Her wavy, long, red hair tumbled down her face as she bent her head to read, and several times she stopped and said, "I can't go on." The supportive silence of everyone in the room formed a safety net under her very young and yet very old small feet. She told her story of how at age 12 she was raped and beaten by the houseboy while her wealthy father and professional mother worked. She was sent to a school for unwed mothers for nine months and then gave the baby up for adoption.

"Maybe I've had my ten kids after that because I always wanted to make up for that loss. I wanted to keep the baby but my mother said, 'No, it'll kill your father.' I mailed him letters from Canada where I was supposed to be but he never knew I was here in the states all the time. He still doesn't know to this day."

She laughed and cried at the same time. Tears streamed down her pale white skin. Someone handed her a toilet tissue roll and she looked up to smile "thank you" and broke into tears again.

Through the body of writing created by the women inmates in the Bright Fires Creative Writing Program at California Rehabilitation Center, (CRC, a medium-security prison, initially designed for people with problems of drug abuse, addiction and drug-related crimes) over the past six years, I have learned about the relationship between child abuse and the incarceration of women.

In 1979, when I began at CRC, I had no idea that at least ninety percent of the women I worked with were victims of child abuse. Nor was I aware that at least seventy-five percent were victims of sexual child abuse.

Child abuse, because it so often leads to self-abuse, has played a major role in the lives of women at CRC. Self-abuse in adulthood may take the form of drug addiction, suicide, mental illness, and/or crime. Thus, child abuse is an integral part of the road to prison for most women with whom I have worked.

A composite of many creative forces was working in the Bright Fires Writing Program at the beginning of 1983. For the first time in their lives, the women involved felt free and safe enough in a group (albeit in prison) to say out loud those words that had been forbidden them in the past. Until now, the taboo of speaking out this demon was too strong. They had been forbidden their voice until finally they didn't know they had one.

The following is a collection of writings from some of these women:

WAR STORIES

Women sharing
    war stories
        that can
only be told here
    behind bars from
        Middle America

War stories
    of prostitution
        nights in labor camps
            not remembering
                how many came

War stories
    about the pain of addiction
        kicking drugs
            after three years running

War stories
    of unwanted abortions
        rapes of children
            that grew to be
                these women

Ryvonne Lewis

A LITTLE GIRL'S QUESTION

She wraps her arms
Tightly around herself
Rocking
Back and forth
Back and forth
Her mind lingers
Tears in her eyes
She can't remember
If daddy came home
But she hears a voice
deep
gruff
"C-mere, honey, sit on Daddy's lap,"
She bounces high
On a sturdy knee
laughing
until the pain
slid up her thigh
"Such a nice little girl,"
Came the sigh . . .

She wraps her arms
Tightly around herself
Rocking
Back and forth
Back and forth
Tears in her eyes
She still can't remember
If Daddy came home . . .

Sandy Slater

SILENT RAGE

My mother died when I was only five days old. Although a very hard task lay ahead for him, my father took the burden of raising me, a girl, all alone.

He knew he couldn't continue without some kind of help, so he hired me out, as he would say, to people who didn't have children of their own.

I guess my father must have felt bad about leaving me with strangers, and one evening he drove up to the house in his big shiny black Oldsmobile and brought me a beautiful teddy bear.

My father told me he was giving Ted E. to me so he could watch out for me while he was away working. I loved Ted E. very much, and told him all of my secrets. We would play for hours, but I wouldn't lay him down because he was not washable.

One fall day I was sitting out on the back porch with Ted E. and squeezing him around the neck very hard, and his head fell off. I ran in the house yelling for someone to "Fix him, fix him." Mr. Akright told me he would fix him, and took me by the hand and led me down the cellar stairs where the furnace was blazing and opened the furnace door. He then took the head of my faithful companion and grabbed me by my hair and, holding my head back, he told me to watch as he threw Ted E.'s head into the flames. I tried to run away from him because I thought he would also throw me in after him. But he held me fast and laughed. This I believe was the first time in my life I ever felt hate.

That night, after I was put to bed, I still felt the rage in my heart. After the door was closed, I took a fist full of my Crayolas and completely covered every inch of walls and furnishings that were in my reach. After I had exhausted myself, I climbed back into the crib and fell fast asleep. I was awakened the next morning by the ranting and raving of Mrs. Akright who was saying how she didn't want such a horrid little girl under her roof. She called my father and when he arrived told him that I was a vicious little girl whom no one would take care of for long.

When we got to the car, my father told me if I always told him the truth that he would be on my side. When I explained to him why I felt I had to do what I did he was very understanding. He didn't spank me, but he told me I should have told him and he would have handled it differently. He did see my side and knew how I must have felt. A few months after this happened they committed Mr. Akright to a mental home where he passed away. To this day I always feel it's better to tell the truth no matter how bad things seem to be.

Pat

DID HE REALLY

"You're no good,"
Aunt Lora would say,
> As young arms would strive
> to shield the young girl from
> blows from the massive woman
>> "You're good,"
>> Uncle Homer said.

"You're evil minded,"
Aunt Lora would say
> When the child would
> ask some naive question
> about something she'd
> heard in school
>> "It's only natural
>> to ask,"
>> Uncle Homer would
>> whisper in hushed
>> tones.

"Until you see the light,"
Aunt Lora would shout
> Slamming the old shed door
> sometimes for days
>> "I brought you
>> something to eat."
>> Uncle Homer would
>> say
>> much later.

"I saw you talking to that new boy
today, you little tramp,"
Aunt Lora would hiss
> Driving home
> the child cringing
> expecting another blow
>> "Boys ain't all
>> bad," Uncle Homer
>> would say.

"Don't expect to hug me,
I don't like to be touched,"
Aunt Lora would pull away
                from any affection
                the child had to offer
                                Uncle Homer loved
                                hugs and kisses.

"Go to the chicken coop and stay,"
Aunt Lora would scream
                as company of
                brothers, cousins and others
                would come on Sunday visits
                                "Wanta go fishing?"
                                Uncle Homer would
                                retrieve
                                her from her
                                feathered
                                prison.

"No one wants you,"
Aunt Lora would bellow
                as the young girl would
                walk into the living room
                                "I want you,"
                                Uncle Homer would
                                say in
                                his slow Southern drawl.

"No one loves you,"
Aunt Lora would insist
                when the girl would
                ask about her
                mother and brother
                                "I love you,"
                                Uncle Homer would say
                                as he gently
                                pulled down
                                her white cotton
                                panties.

Ryvonne

WILL THE REAL CRIMINAL
PLEASE STAND UP

She was six
He was thirty

She was a child with raven hair
and ivory skin

Fragile innocence
a young princess like you'd meet
in Brothers Grimm

     Except

he caught her
held back her flailing arms,
tore at her party dress
inserted pain

For years she lived in paralysis
afraid for anyone to touch her
she imagined spiders
and other crawling things
living inside her

at eight

    at nine

       at ten

again and again
she cried Momma, Momma,
He whispered, "I'll kill you if you tell."

till one day she found him
with her sister
she told her Grandma
who hit him on the head with a frying pan
till he grew into a monster
and threw the ninety year old woman out the window

   she died soon after

the little girl escaped
years later she found PCP
her drug of choice to kill the pain

married
  frigid
    insane
     and Norman?

   He is still free.

Sharon Sticker

The taboo against speaking about child abuse, especially sexual abuse, has been so great that the victims have lost their own voices. They have been told, "Don't tell or I'll kill." They have been forced to swallow their own voices and thus to lose or negate an essential part of themselves.

As a result I came to understand very clearly my role in this prison. There was a great need to discover this lost, forgotten or hidden voice. The gift of creative writing became the tool for this exploration and communication. We learned to talk to each other in writing, to break the silence, to tell secrets.

The expiation of repressed guilt, blame, rage, and sorrow after so many years was critical for any growth or change. People need the mourning and a compassionate listener. They need rituals for imaginative confrontations with their fear of speaking out, or a workshop setting which allows them to release their own voice, thereby releasing the voices of others. The whole atmosphere of repression is lifted.

The notion of the voice, the ability to express all the feelings and emotions that have been repressed due to this childhood trauma, is the important key here. It has been with the lifting of the voice through the creation of a work of art in the form of prose, poetry, or dramatic dialogue and the subsequent presentation of this art form to the larger public that has served to free many of the women with whom I have worked. These were points of transformation. No one was ever the same after this. Many who went through this process are on their way to healing.

Sharon Sticker
Director
Bright Fires Creative Writing Program
California Rehabilitation Center

INSIGHTS AND PERCEPTIONS

Stepping into the light is an experience we all long for. Along the continuum of healing, the light becomes brighter the longer and harder you strive for recovery. We wish we had a magic wand to take away your hurt and make everything good, but there is no magic to be found in this process. It is a journey that lasts a lifetime. We know that a stronger person with a deeper understanding of life emerges from going through each step of the struggle.

You cannot ever change what happened to you, but we believe you have the power and the ability to choose what you do with what did happen. Once you deal with your emotions, you can begin to integrate them into your total life. This integration process does not mean you no longer remember the past or feel the feelings; instead you are freed to remember and feel. Start now to rewrite the outcome of your life story.

The experiences, the visions, and the effects of the abuse will fade away, but not completely. There will always be faded memories. As you gather in the healing light, you will triumph over darkness.

BE VICTORIOUS

HEALING PROCESS

*"Sometimes I am guiding with a light touch, some-
times pulling, sometimes pushing but only so far as
they are able to move at the time . . . I see the goodness
they cannot yet feel."*

Vicki Heuer Dagle, M.S.W.

SEARCHING FOR TRUST

Perhaps the most difficult stumbling block in an adult victim's recovery from childhood incest and abuse is the lack of someone to trust — someone who will be there through the thick and thin of recovery and who will rejoice when it is time to be free to fly on your own wings. The struggle and search for this type of support system can leave one feeling rejected, hopeless, and alone.

While we commend the support that is rapidly growing for children who have been victimized, there continues to be little assistance for adult victims, who search for some sort of "normalcy" within their own lives. As the years pass, and the secret gets forced deeper and deeper into the victim's inner core, the ability to open up and trust someone is much more difficult. However, there comes a time, whether today or next year, when the secret within cries to be let out. Then begins the search for someone to trust.

The purpose here is to give some specific guidelines for this process of finding someone to trust. One needs to spend time and energy on healing rather than on searching for a therapist. The following case study is an example of the trials one adult victim of child sexual abuse had to go through to get the help she so desperately needed.

Sara: A case study

Sara, a victim of multiple abuses from her earliest years, had gotten to a point where she was no longer able to separate the past from the present. Everything that went on in her life, as an adult, reminded her of the past she kept trying to forget.

She had no memory of the abuses that tormented her for many years; they were merely "nightmares" or "clouded images" that she didn't relate to any personal life experiences. Continual mood swings left her suicidal, self-destructive, frustrated, angry, repulsed, and disgusted. She had forgotten how to cry, laugh, and live . . . if she ever really knew. She hid within a world that she alone had created, and feared leaving her home to do even the simplest chores. Trapped, she panicked and felt that she would no longer be able to go on.

Sara had unconsciously been looking for someone to whom she could tell her secret for many, many years. She remembered more than once being called into the vice principal's office for misbehaving in school. But no one ever asked, no one ever heard the internal cries of a ten-year-old girl, and she didn't know how to put into words what was really going on in her life. "Dad touches me where he shouldn't," or "Grandfather makes me kiss him funny when I sit on his lap." No one ever saw the signs that were written on her face.

At age 12, Sara's mother took her to a psychiatrist at the request of the school. He told her that they would be good friends as he started to make advances towards her.

Her first year in college, 3,000 miles away from home, Sara tried to kill herself. She was shuffled off to the confines of the University Medical Center where she was asked a lot of questions, given a couple of tests and never, never once, asked why she tried to do it.

Later that year in another attempt to kill herself, Sara first called the college hotline. She spoke with the director of the Counseling Center, who encouraged her to come over and talk. They talked, and he listened sensitively, and quickly referred her to another counselor. With this person she spent two years talking about why she hated school, why she couldn't stand her roommates, and her dreams of marriage to a knight on a white horse who would make everything better. After two years of this she was referred to a local mental health clinic because, as the therapist said, "I couldn't deal with the slowness of Sara's pace in therapy. We never seemed to work a problem through without having to go back to the beginning and work through it all over again."

An additional two years were spent with a psychiatrist talking about her "avoidance of sexual discussions," as he put it. By this time she had gone through three different types of group therapy focusing on a variety of nonrelated topics, including assertiveness, socialization, and women's issues. Never once in her entire time of therapy did anyone ever mention sexual abuse. Sara's problem was variously diagnosed as depression, borderline personality, manic-depressive, psychosis, hysteria, and miriad other catch-all phrases.

One morning after three months of a never-ending roller coaster ride on drugs and alcohol mixed with confusion, self-mutilating behavior and personal turmoil, Sara realized she could not take the volcano that was building inside her anymore. Making a "planned escape," Sara began to swallow the pills she had stored away in vitamin bottles for some time. This escape had been long planned in fine detail, but never completely carried out — "Until today," she thought. There seemed to be no way out but death. The future looked hopeless, and Sara didn't know how to go on with the facade of living anymore.

Before passing out, Sara called a local women's hotline and they saw that she was taken to the emergency room of a nearby hospital. Released four hours later, she returned home with nothing accomplished and no one to take care of her.

It was at this point, in a moment of clarity, that Sara realized she had to find someone to trust. She made a list of what she wanted out of her life, her marriage, her world, and she decided that no matter how long it would take, or how frightening it would be, she would go in search of someone who could help her find the answers to her own life questions. Being a person who believed in prayer, she prayed for God to provide her with a solution, someone to listen, someone to learn from, someone with whom she could share.

Sara found that person. After years of searching frantically for life and help she found someone ready to listen. She found a therapist who would support her and allow her to grow, building trust at a pace that she could handle. But life had just begun. Still there were the suicidal intentions, and the multitude of feelings she had to confront. After watching and working with her for more than a year and a half, her therapist finally asked, "Sara, have you ever been sexually abused?" And then the work really began. But she had, at last, found someone to work with her, someone to trust, someone to show her the reasons to go on, and someone to fight for her.

The point of this case study is that counseling cannot merely focus on one aspect of the client, such as acting-out behavior, self-abuse, or suicidal thoughts. A therapist has to be willing to look beyond all of that and see the person as a whole — the whole body, mind, and spirit.

While each client-counselor partnership is different and unique, there are some basic qualities inherent in all therapists who have the potential to become someone to trust. Some points to remember:

1. Look for someone with experience.

The length and extent of the therapist's education is not a major factor. Anyone with a Ph.D., M.S., or pastoral counseling degree is just as qualified to work on the variety of topics needing exploration as someone with an M.D. The only significant difference, besides salary, status, and counseling theories, is that an M.D. may directly prescribe medications, whereas other therapists must rely on the occasional support of physicians for medical management of drugs.

What is important is that the counselor you see has expertise that relates to you and your problems. Check out specific counselors by getting referrals from people you feel you can trust. People who have been through similar experiences can offer valuable insights.

2. Trust yourself.

Call and make an intake appointment with the therapist you have chosen. Go trusting your own intuition and gut-level feelings to let you know whether or not this is someone you can work with. You are your own best indicator. Use this time to meet the counselor, discuss basic issues you would be interested in working on, and "interview" him or her. Be prepared to ask specific questions that may be pertinent to you, i.e., cost, personal beliefs, type of training in certain areas of expertise, what rules the therapist adheres to in the course of therapy. You have the right to answers delivered in a straightforward and honest manner.

Remember, you are the one who is commissioning the counselor to join in your journey toward recovery.

After the session, allow yourself time to think. Is this someone you could work with in the closeness of a therapeutic relationship? Do they seem preoccupied, or do they present a manner that makes you feel comfortable and safe? Do they have patience? Is the therapist humble, having the ability to learn, while being confident in his/her own skills? Is there room for play within the course of therapy, and does the therapist have a good sense of humor? Are they willing to be there for you during times of crisis for phone calls and/or extra session time if needed?

Do not feel bound to return to a counselor just because you feel the person was nice to you, or that you have to take care of the counselor's needs. Remember, you are there to work on your own issues. If you feel trapped into meeting their needs and "getting well" for them, the time spent in therapy will be lost. It is quite easy for adult victims of abuse to fall back into the caretaking roles they were placed in when the original abuse occurred.

3. Seek empathy.

One of a therapist's most important qualities is the ability to respond with empathy. This does not mean they have to have shared the same life experiences, but they must be able to understand how you feel — as if they were the client. Then they can come to a full understanding of the problem and work from a more objective view when it comes to problem-solving.

It is very important that the therapist be willing to self-disclose and share some of their own life experiences with the client. These experiences help the therapist relate to where the client is emotionally at the time, while providing a different view of understanding for the client. Allowing a time of open, honest, genuine sharing is an indication that a counselor is trustworthy.

4. Establish communication.

There should always be active communication between client and therapist. Modern counseling is a two-way process. If something is not working, be willing to tell your therapist that, and search together for a means to get things moving again. Both counselor and client have to be willing to be flexible so that the best therapy is obtained for the client.

5. Develop support structures outside of therapy.

Rarely does the counseling session truly end when the client walks out of the office. There are always more thoughts to deal with and feelings to be discussed. It is very important that the client go about developing positive support structures outside of therapy. This type of support can be especially helpful when dealing with emotionally charged topics. Surround yourself with people who, while they might not know the whole picture, have some idea what is going on in your life and are willing to give unconditional support and care. Therapy is quite emotionally draining, and the better the support system, the faster the recovery time.

Often group therapy, in conjunction with individual counseling, provides this much-needed supportive atmosphere. Within a group setting, you can begin to establish outside support systems with others who will be able to relate to your experiences and to understand and validate your struggles.

6. Make your decision for recovery.

Once you have found a therapist you can trust, you yourself have to make the decision that you are ready and willing to work on your own issues. The courage to take this step does not come easily. It often appears to the client that the risks involved in opening to healing far outweigh the advantages. One has to grapple with fears of change, of processing through pain, and of the implications of recovery for family and friends. It will take all your willingness to grow and stretch yourself through constant self-examination. The process toward healing may seem slow, tedious, and tiresome; it will be intermingled with periods of self-doubt, denial, and fear. However, the rewards are worth it all! Recovery!

Editor's note: The following material on victims' reactions is presented in a generalized format. However, we caution you not to look at all this information as either dark or light, with no shades of gray. Life isn't that way. Every assault situation was a real event; if you were the victim, it has left its mark on you, as a child and as an adult. The worst response to this material would be to say, "After reading this I guess my experience wasn't that big of a deal, so what am I making all the fuss about?" We repeat: if it happened to you, it happened 100 percent!!

How Children React

A child victim's reaction to sexual assault depends on a lot of factors:

1. What is the relationship between the child and the molester? The closer the molester is to the child and the family unit, the greater the trauma. If the molester is a total stranger, the long-term effects will be less.
2. How many times did the sexual assault occur? The greater the number, the greater the trauma. A single assault seems to be easier for a child to deal with than multiple assaults over a long period of time.
3. How much force or violence was used on the child during the assault? Again, the more violent the attack, the greater the child's emotional reaction to the assault.
4. Was emotional abuse — especially shame, guilt and/or embarrassment — used as a tactic to sexually assault the child? The answer to this question is almost always yes, and this results in greater emotional reactions and long-term effects on the child.

The amount of trauma the child experienced can be directly related to these and perhaps other issues. Child victims of sexual assault may be expected to exhibit any or all of the following negative reactions: sleep and eating problems, fear of school, emotional regression, depression, suicidal thoughts (yes, even in children!), physical symptomology, shock, and bed-wetting.

For Adult Incest Survivors

Many people do not realize the long-lasting effects incest can have on children. Even into their adulthood, victims carry an immense amount of very intense feelings. The same negative reactions that were listed above for children can persist into their adult lives. For many, the trauma of the abuse has been buried away even to the point of forgetting that it ever happened. When this occurs, the symptoms are the same, but no one can put all the pieces together. Only after the nightmares of the abuse are confronted can recovery take place.

The following is a list of some of the feelings victims typically experience and some of the comments that accompany these feelings:

1. **Loss of control:** "My whole life is falling apart. Why am I so powerless?" Or, "I need someone to put me back together again."
2. **Loss of feelings:** "I don't feel anything, I am numb." And, "I think I have forgotten how to cry."
3. **Fear:** "I know I am not safe; he is going to come back and get me again." And, "I think I am going crazy." Or, "The nightmares I have overwhelm me." And, "Is it ever going to be the way it was before all this happened?"
4. **Anxiety:** "I can't breathe, I am really nervous." Or, "I just want to eat and eat and eat." Or, "I can't go outside anymore; it really scares me to be there." And "I feel like my stomach is all tied up in knots."
5. **Anger:** "I hate him so very much, I could just kill him." "All men are alike; the only thing they want you for is sex." And, "I feel like Mt. St. Helens is going to erupt inside me at any moment."
6. **Denial:** "I was lying, nothing really happened." Or, "What happened to me wasn't that big a deal." Or, "I just made the whole thing up." And, "I was just lying to get some attention."
7. **Confusion:** "I don't really know what happened to today; it just kind of disappeared." Or, "I'm feeling overwhelmed and having trouble focusing on my day-to-day chores." And, "It seems like the abuse just happened today when I really know it happened long ago."

8. **Depression:** "I am doing nothing but crying all the time." Or, "Everything is just hopeless; I'm too tired to fight this anymore." And, "I think about killing myself every day!"

9. **Helplessness:** "I can't do what you expect me to do, I am just not capable."

10. **Self-mutilation:** "I feel like I need to cut myself just to release the tension that builds up inside of me. Once I have cut, things seem to feel a whole lot better."

11. **Shame:** "I have to take five showers a day, and wash my hands hundreds of times because I feel so dirty."

12. **Guilt:** "I just know it was all my fault. Maybe if I had done something different it would never have happened." Or, "He told me he had to do it because I was so very, very bad. I should have been a better child."

Editor's note: Annette Selmer, M.S., and Kao Rhiannon, Ph.D., are both therapists in Portland, Oregon, who assist women and men through their healing processes.

A FRAMEWORK FOR TREATMENT

As mental health therapists, and as women in this society, we have become increasingly aware of the core themes in the lives of the people with whom we are privileged to work. These themes are pervasive among people who have experienced sexual molestation during their childhood and adolescence. The following discussion will bring together some observations that may help provide a clearer sense of how a journey towards reclaiming losses in one's life might unfold.

To begin with, what do we now know about sexual abuse? Not only is the healthy developmental progression impeded by abuse, but the feelings of vulnerability and powerlessness our society already fosters in women and children are accentuated. Abuse reinforces the ways in which women and children have learned to devalue themselves.

We define sexual abuse as a developmental disruption that is manifested by another person's acting out sexually exploitive behaviors toward a person with less power and more vulnerability. It is a sexually oriented activity intended to stimulate the perpetrator, with disregard for the emotional and physical consequences to the victim. People who have been victimized are not in any way responsible for the abuse.

Sexual abuse happens in numerous ways. Many people have been sexually abused by more than one person. Sexual abuse ranges from covert abuse, such as uncomfortable looks, innuendoes, exploitive attitudes and behaviors, and touching, to overt abuse such as rape, fondling, and instances of group exploitiveness.

When people have been overtly abused, they can often describe that behavior and attach feelings to those certain acts. Covert abuse often makes a victim feel "crazy" because there is usually no actual behavior to describe. Rather, covert abuse involves a feeling, an intuition, or a sense. This kind of abuse, while just as emotionally painful, often gets ignored, overlooked, or discounted.

You might ask, "Why would I want to do all this work?" Our answer is that you deserve it! You deserve to have a life open to options rather than closed off by rigid armor. You deserve a chance to check out with yourself which defenses are still necessary and which you can discard.

Therapy does not mean that all these advances will happen at once. Responsible therapy is a slow and careful process that is done with you, not to you, at a rate you can handle and control. You need to be in charge of your own therapy (with the exception of self-destructive actions towards yourself or others, and other issues regarding health and safety). It is inherent in the therapy process that some control be turned over to the therapist. However, we believe that before that happens, each client should have in mind a framework for treatment.

Prior to dealing with the issues it is important to address and seek help for current violent relationships, drug and alcohol dependencies, eating disorders, and other health and safety problems.

Up to this point we have provided some information on why you might want treatment. Now we will discuss the stages of the treatment process in a linear way. But remember, each person goes through this process in their own way and pace with their own degree of intensity.

PHASES OF TREATMENT

1. "Call for help"
Something happens in a person's life that brings abuse related issues to the forefront. For example, the death of a family member, the birth of a child, seeing a movie, a friend going into treatment, recovery from chemical dependency, etc., may trigger your feelings about previous traumatic experiences.

Entering therapy can be frightening and often involves feelings of panic, suicidal impulses, or feeling overly vulnerable. Again, the degrees of vulnerability and fear will vary from person to person.

2. "Telling"
What can ensue if, instead of repressing or pushing down the trauma even deeper, you decide to tell someone about it? This can be a very scary experience for many reasons. Telling begins to make what happened to you more "real." For

At this phase people want to talk about their abuse a lot. It is very important to have appropriate people around to listen, plus a trusted therapist to guide you and offer suggestions for protection from self.

Preoccupied with their abuse, many people become fearful that they will lose their familiar selves. A frequent reaction at this time, in contrast to confusion and being overwhelmed, is hyperalertness and hypervigilance.

5. "Transition Phase"

At some point your resurfacing emotions begin to come together with the information you have been receiving in a way that begins to make sense. Survivors become aware that they have acted out some of their worst fears around losing control, feelings, remembering, and telling others. Yet they have begun to find new coping strategies that work. You now begin using more appropriate, less self-destructive, coping and defensive styles.

6. "Personal Growth"

At this phase people are much more present and future oriented. While the past is seen as affecting the present and future, it is no longer confused with the present. People look at their patterns, their needs and dreams and aspirations, and determine ways to get what they want from life. Not only do they begin to get a clearer sense of who they are, but who they are in relation to others, as well. They are able to develop more spontaneity in their lives. Thoughts and decisions now are rarely based on fear.

7. "Integration"

Here people are able to integrate their past experiences, seeing who they are and who they have the potential to become. Fears no longer guide their lives; memories do not control or ruin a day. Life is seen as a series of options rather than a series of controlling influences.

PARAMETERS FOR TREATMENT

When entering a process similar to the one we have described, we highly suggest certain parameters to ensure your emotional safety. First, select a therapist who is familiar with this therapy process. They should have information to give you about sexual abuse and other early childhood traumas, such as familial alcoholism, stress disorders, and dysfunctional families. The therapist should be aware of how difficult and courageous it is to consider entering a therapeutic process. The therapist needs to be well trained not only in sexual abuse treatment for adults, but also concerning treatment of alcoholism and chemical dependency. If necessary, he or she should be able to pick up on warning or danger signs in you and help you get an assessment, accurate information, and treatment. If you are using stimulants or depressants, whether prescription or street drugs, at the same time that you are attempting to go through therapy, you are working at cross-purposes with yourself on many levels. You are then working for and against health, for and against control, as well as for and against feeling.

Another health issue to address prior to this process is eating disorders. These include starving, excessive exercising, compulsive and/or binge eating, and purging with laxatives or vomiting. Appropriate resolution of these issues is critical prior to and during therapy.

Additionally, the issues of physical and/or emotional violence in your life need to be addressed. This behavior includes violence from others toward the survivor, and the survivor's violence toward others. As people go through the emotional upheaval of healing, they need to know that they, and others around them, are safe.

Once you have used a selection process to choose a knowledgeable and receptive therapist, it is our belief that together you should negotiate a commitment to therapy. Then stick to that commitment, even though your impulses may be to not show up for appointments. We recommend an initial 10 to 12 week commitment with weekly and (occasional bi-weekly) sessions. Together with this, group therapy is extremely useful. In our opinion, group therapy should not occur without adjunctive individual therapy.

OUTCOME

The healing process does not entail becoming a new person. Rather, it means letting go of those parts of you that were holding you back and stifling your creative energy. Because there is a letting go, healing is a grief process. But you can retain and honor the qualities that helped you survive such horrible ordeals in your life.

As you overcome past traumas, you let go of unrealistic expectations, and commit to a healthier, safer existence. Admit to yourself that you are worthy and deserving, that you are as important as anyone else, no matter what your family or the perpetrators think. You have the right to be healthier than the family from which you came! When you no longer sacrifice yourself for others, it does not mean you do not care for others, but rather that you will not do so at your own expense.

CONCLUSION

Guiding people through this journey has had an extreme impact on our lives as therapists. We have admired the strength and courage of people who have risen above horrors far beyond that which we previously believed people could survive emotionally and physically.

Within each of us is a hurt child, symbolic of the child we used to be. Everyone's heart has been broken in some way at some time. It isn't fair when someone's heart gets broken so young, so abruptly, or so cruelly and so senselessly.

While such realization has brought tears over the unfairness and injustices inflicted on others, it has primarily brought us a sense of renewal. We have watched people's lives expand into that which they might have been if they had never been hurt.

It has been a gift to watch the emerging of our clients' hearts, souls, bodies, and intellects through their talk, writing, dreams, art, decisions, activities, and more. Their accomplishments give us hope for all the others who have not yet found the way to reach out. They give us hope for all the people who have reached out and who do feel clearer and better about themselves and their lives. They give us hope for the future generations. The beginning of societal change often starts on such a very personal level.

Editor's note: Vicki Heuer Dagle, M.S.W. is a Registered Clinical Social Worker specializing in the treatment of sexual abuse victims for the past ten years.

COMING INTO THE LIGHT

What are we doing to our children? I have worked with women and children for over ten years, crying and laughing with them as we walked together through the darkness. Sometimes I am guiding with a light touch, sometimes pulling, sometimes pushing, but only so far as they are able to move at the time. We walk, run, rest, play, laugh, and weep. I am humble in the presence of those on this journey, as their courage surpasses comprehension.

What are we doing to our children? We must realize that this is not just the problem of some sick or perverted people. This is not just the problem of the children who are victimized. This is a toxin that is pervasive throughout our culture and must be addressed in a real and direct way by all of us. The question above not only refers to little girls who are victimized, but also to little boys who grow up in a world of ridicule and abuse. They are taught to hide their hurt, shame, and humiliation. Their only acceptable release of emotion is through anger; their only pathway to love and intimacy is through their sexuality. They learn how to use sex as a way to be powerful and to release their own pent-up emotions on someone less powerful.

We will not remove this toxin from our society, unless we address the whole picture. Up to now, we have begun to acknowledge the problem and are learning to help those who have been victimized heal from their childhood traumas. Now we must deal with the patterns that not only create victims, but also offenders.

It is necessary to look at the childhood of the offender to understand the cycle of abuse. With this understanding, changes can be made that will break the cycle from one generation to another. It is my hope we can all begin the process of healing universally by becoming very aware and knowledgeable about the problem. Public education is an entry point. The solution also lies in how we view our children while they are growing up. We must begin to know that they are people with rights and deserve to be respected. If we do not treat them as such when they are young, how can they know of their goodness when they are older?

What are we doing to our children? I have been privileged to facilitate and guide some of those who are on their path toward healing their childhood traumas. I marvel at their strength and courage. I see the goodness they cannot yet feel. I reflect that goodness back to them and surround them in it and slowly, tentatively, cautiously, they begin to feel the warmth. The warmth brings light inside the body and their eyes begin to open, allowing them to see themselves as I see them — innocent, wonderful children deserving of love, nurturance, and kindness. They then begin to venture forward toward the light, toward the realization of their goodness, toward self-acceptance and love, and finally toward forgiveness. This is the journey. It cannot be rushed and no short-cuts can be taken. Attempts to leap to forgiveness of others before forgiving self are self-injurious. Attempts to forget the past before telling its secrets only bury the wounds deeper and continue the pain to the body and psyche.

Finally, though we have not personally experienced sexual abuse nor had it touch our own families, we must not assume that it is not our concern or our problem. Each of us has our own childhood pains that we have a *responsibility* to resolve, so that we can indeed love our children unconditionally and thereby truly break the cycle of abuse.

Editor's note: *the following guidance was offered to a fifteen-year-old girl who had been raped by her stepfather.*

RELEASE YOUR TORMENTOR

What is important is not so much what you have to say, but how you feel. Feelings are something I understand. Words were created only to express the emotions within one's soul.

You are in a bit of a conflict, and you are needing direction. I will give you some guidance and help open some doors for you. But remember, all that is ever important is how you feel.

Now understand this: with respect to your tormentor, he despises himself for the act. Yet, you are now tormenting yourself by your hurt and anger. Release your tormentor, who is you, and begin to be a little girl again.

In your society, little girls have been encouraged to look like women who would tempt the heart of any man. But little girls should *stay* little girls for a long time. The same goes for little boys. But here, everything is rushed. Here, children grow up in great conflict, for they don't know what they are supposed to be or how they are supposed to look. If they look anything other than the accepted mode, they are afraid they will be rejected. If they do not act as their peers or parents want them to act, they feel they will not be loved. What a travesty! And here, there are fathers who abuse their daughters, molest them, and do many things to them to prove they are still young and virile men, because in your society and its limited thinking, "youth" is *all* that matters. I find that abominable!

Please understand this: the one who has hurt you is also a child of this society and its direful consciousness. As little boys grow up, they are told to be certain ways, to act certain ways; it is programmed into their beings, so it becomes a part of their consciousness in attitude. And they are always esteemed if they are young and agile and rich. But when their age begins to show and their potency is questioned, often they will turn to young women in order to madly hold on to something they feel they are losing, because they want to be loved and accepted. The same is true with women.

You are a little girl. Yet you don't even know what it's like to be a little girl, because from the time you were a young child your life has been the product of rushing to become a grown-up.

Be a little girl and do what the child inside you wishes to do. Make all your dreams come true. Allow yourself to grow gracefully into womanhood rather than running into it. And always keep the child-like simplicity that allows you to love everyone.

If others are adorning themselves to look the image of a woman, do not imitate them. Simply be what you are. Then you will keep your youth a long time, and you will find happiness, extraordinary happiness, but not until you release this.

In ancient times men were hacked to bits for doing what your father did. Their heads were cut off and flung into the sea. But that never helped anyone. In a very real sense, nothing has been taken away from you unless you feel that it has. Understand that. Love yourself and forgive the one who has hurt you. This does not mean you must stay with him. But forgive him and forgive yourself, and earnestly love and adore who you are. You are worth all the love you can give to yourself.

What has happened in your past is over. It is no longer of importance. Do not allow scars to rest within your being. There is no need for them to be there. Do not allow your life to be marred by another's hatred of himself, ever. For then you are victimizing your own being. No one is worth the feelings of bitterness or anger.

Whatever words you can speak can do very little to represent your emotions, and I understand that. Your emotions are not marred; they are still beautiful. For your sake — and no one else's — keep them that way; keep the fire burning brightly within your being. Look upon your being and see it as precious, and never lose that image. And never lower yourself by despising anyone. Then the love within you will add to your beauty, and you will be a gem beyond measure and, one day, you'll have a sweet and gentle relationship.

I will help you to find some friends who will be joyous and happy. Be happy with them. And one day, when your mother can shake loose from her material securities, you can both go away to a place where you will find extraordinary peace, which is worth much more than any material value that has been gained through this relationship.

There once was an age for adolescence, and it went through one's thirty-third year. Try earnestly to be a child until you are at least 33. Then you will have lived, enjoyed, gained wisdom; you will have learned of evenness, compassion, humility, and who you are. I believe you will never age if you do this, and you will always keep your youthful appearance.

You are greatly loved, lass. Go and run in your fields and have laughter. So be it.

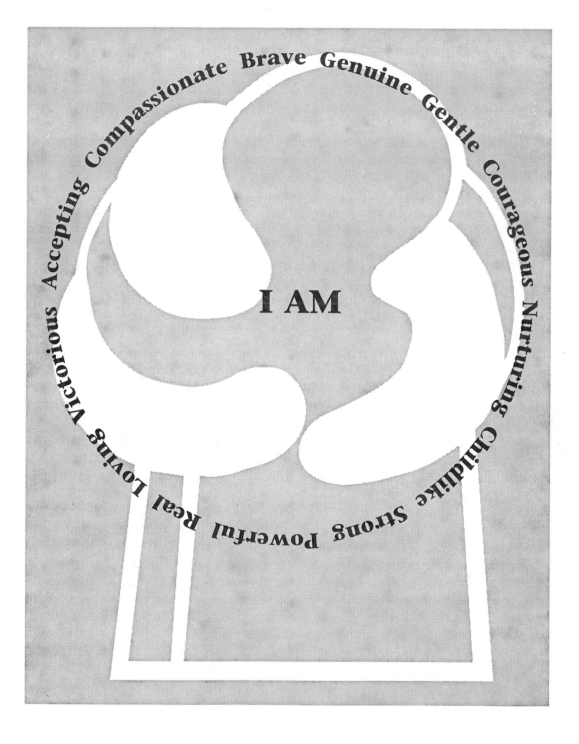

I AM

Accepting Compassionate Brave Genuine Gentle Courageous Nurturing Childlike Strong Powerful Real Loving Victorious

A P P E N D I X

SUGGESTED READING

Incest and Sexuality: *A Guide to Understanding and Healing*
Maltz, Wendy; Holman, Beverly, 1987 (Massachusetts: Lexington Books).
Gives insight into how incest survivors' sexuality is affected by the abuse, and provides practical, positive steps on how a healthy sexual attitude can be developed.

A Sourcebook on Child Sexual Abuse
Finkelhor, David, 1986 (Beverly Hills, Calif.: Sage Publications).
Discusses in detail the prevalence of child sexual abuse, and the initial and long-term effects of the trauma; also provides information regarding offenders.

Surviving Sexual Assault
Edited by: Grossman, Rochel and Sutherland, Joan, 1983 (New York: Congdon & Weed, Inc.).
An excellent booklet that provides tips on rape prevention and assault survivor information. Includes a limited nationwide directory of treatment agencies.

I Never Told Anyone: *Writings By Women Survivors of Child Sexual Abuse*
Bass, Ellen; Thornton, Louise, 1983 (New York: Harper/Colophon Books).
Excerpts of writings by adult incest survivors who share their feelings and their stories after attending workshops given by the authors.

Father-Daughter Incest
Herman, Judith Lewis, 1981 (Cambridge, Mass.: Harvard University Press).
An excellent overview for victims of father-daughter incest. Covers a wide scope of research and treatment issues.

No More Secrets: *Protecting Your Child From Sexual Assault*
Adams, Caren; Fay, Jennifer, 1981 (San Luis Obispo, Calif.: Impact Publishers).
A short, understandable book for every parent to read and use to help educate their children on sexual assault and its prevention.

The Best Kept Secret
Rush, Florence, 1980 (Englewood Cliffs, N.J.: Prentice Hall).
An overwhelming historical overview of the sexual abuse of children and the victimization of children.

The Silent Children: *A Parent's Guide to the Prevention of Child Sexual Abuse*
Sanford, Linda Tschirhart, 1980 (New York: McGraw-Hill Book Company).
Teaches parents important facts about instructing their children and thereby preventing child sexual abuse.

Conspiracy of Silence: *The Trauma of Incest*
Butler, Sandra, 1978 (San Francisco: New Glide Publishers).
Provides a close examination of all those affected by the trauma of incest, including the victim, the offender, the non-offending parent, and the family as a unit.

Betrayal of Innocence
Forward, Susan; Buck, Craig, 1978 (New York: Penguin Books).
Reviews the history, dynamics and case studies of various types of incestuous relationships including mother, father, and sibling incest.

INVITATION TO AUTHORS

Besides our continued commitment to work in the area of sexual abuse, we are also interested in gathering material regarding emotional and spiritual recovery from satanic ritual abuse. If you would like to share some of your experiences, feelings and an account of your own recovery process for use in future publications, please send your work* and a self-addressed stamped envelope to *ECHOES* at the address below.

NEWSLETTER

To obtain additional writings we have received since the publication of this book, please send a self-addressed stamped envelope (required for any reply) and $2.00 to cover *ECHOES NETWORK, Inc.*, newsletter printing fees. If we do not gather enough entries to print a newsletter, we will return your money in your self-addressed stamped envelope. Please allow six to eight weeks to hear from us.

Send to:

ECHOES NETWORK, Inc.
Newsletter
P.O. Box 06163
Portland, OR 97206

* To insure the protection of each author all material will be kept in strict confidence. No material will be used without the expressed written consent of the author.

NETWORKING SERVICES

Because there is such limited support in adult recovery, and so many people searching for help and understanding, we want to offer some networking possibilities to our readers.

For professional organizations: If you are affiliated with an organization or support group that works with adult survivors of abuse and you would like to have your services (individual counseling, group therapy, crisis lines, service organizations, shelter homes, in-patient care, etc.) added into our networking computer, please send us: the name of your organization, contact person, address, phone number, a brief outline of services available, and $5.00 to cover computer fees.

For child and adult survivors: If you would like a list of networking resources available near you, please send a self-addressed stamped envelope (including your zip code), and $1.00 for computer fees.

Send to:
ECHOES NETWORK, Inc.
Networking Services
P.O. Box 06163
Portland, OR 97206

With Much Care And Support!

Wendy and Leslie

Other Books of Interest Available From
Beyond Words Publishing, Inc.

Seeing Beyond 20-20 by Dr. Robert-Michael Kaplan

An internationally noted authority in vision training gives readers a practical, solidly researched 21-day program for self-help in working towards clearer
vision. Dr. Kaplan, who was himself plagued with double vision, combines clinical
evidence with case examples, the theory of whole-brain perception and the wisdom of alternative therapies from around the world. Topics covered include
nutrition and aerobics for the eyes, losing vision fitness, the eyes as a biofeedback
device, the relationship of inner vision to outer sight and more.

$12.95
soft cover

Healing The Whole Person, The Whole Planet

For the first time, eighteen spirit teachers have gathered to give readers
channeled information about health on a personal and global level. Their wisdom
and insight provides tools for eliminating disease and the causes of illness and
distress. Other topics covered include healing, maintaining health, the integration of body, mind and spirit, AIDS, and the relationship of individual and plane-
tary health.

$12.95
soft cover

Inspiring Days

A perpetual calender containing refreshing, positive and inspirational thoughts
and images. Inspiring Days is never out of date and can be used year after year.
It makes a perfect gift for friends, loved ones or business associates. Three
hundred sixty six different thoughts to inspire your day.

$7.95

Beyond Words publishes books for adults and children. For a free catalog of Beyond Words Publishing titles, please write or call.

BEYOND WORDS PUBLISHING, Inc.
Pumpkin Ridge Road
Rt. 3, Box 492 B
Hillsboro, OR 97123
503-647-5109
Toll Free: 1-800-284-9673

To order by mail, include $2.50 per book for shipping and handling. Enclose a check or money order; or give us a Visa, MasterCard or American Express number, expiration date, and a daytime phone number.

NOTES